Supernatural Attraction and Co-Creation

By

Jeremy Lopez

Supernatural Attraction and Co-Creation

By Dr. Jeremy Lopez

Copyright © 2020

This book is licensed solely for your personal enjoyment only. This book may not be re-sold or given away to other people. If you would like to share this book with another person, please purchase an additional copy for each recipient. If you're reading this book and you did not purchase it or it was not purchased for your use only, please return to your favorite book retailer and purchase your own copy.

All rights reserved. This book is protected under the copyright laws of the United States of America. This book may not be copied or reprinted for commercial gain or profit. The use of short quotations or occasional page copying for personal or group study is permitted and encouraged.

Published by Identity Network

P.O. Box 38213

Birmingham, AL 35238

www.IdentityNetwork.net

ENDORSEMENTS

"You are put on this earth with incredible potential and a divine destiny. This powerful, practical man shows you how to tap into power you didn't even know you had." – Brian Tracy – Author, *The Power of Self Confidence*

"I found myself savoring the concepts of the Law of Attraction merging with the Law of Creativity until slowly the beautiful truths seeped deeper into my thirsty soul. I am called to be a Creator! My friend, Dr. Jeremy Lopez, has a way of reminding us of our eternal 'I-Amness' while putting the tools in our hands to unlock our endless creative potential with the Divine mind. As a

musical composer, I'm excited to explore, with greater understanding, the infinite realm of possibilities as I place fingers on my piano and whisper, 'Let there be!'" – Dony McGuire, Grammy Award winning artist and musical composer

"Jeremy dives deep into the power of consciousness and shows us that we can create a world where the champion within us can shine and how we can manifest our desires to live a life of fulfillment. A must read!" – Greg S. Reid – Forbes and Inc. top rated Keynote Speaker

"I have been privileged to know Jeremy Lopez for many years, as well as sharing the platform with him at a number of conferences. Through this time, I have found him as a man of integrity,

commitment, wisdom, and one of the most networked people I have met. Jeremy is an entrepreneur and a leader of leaders. He has amazing insights into leadership competencies and values. He has a passion to ignite this latent potential within individuals and organizations and provide ongoing development and coaching to bring about competitive advantage and success. I would highly recommend him as a speaker, coach, mentor, and consultant." – Chris Gaborit – Learning Leader, Trainer

CONTENTS

Preface	p.1
Introduction	p.7
Supernatural Attraction	p.21
Progression	p.43
That Which Was Lost	p.65
As a Man Thinketh	p.89
What's in a Name?	p.109
The Visible and Invisible	p.129
Conscious Versus Un-Conscious	p.151
The Glory	p.169
Closing Thoughts	p.187

ACKNOWLEDGMENTS

This book is dedicated to the many, many seekers of God throughout the world who, like me, have a passion to better know the matchless glory of the Kingdom within us. To every seeker and lover of God determined to lay claim to the abundant life, the abundant life is well within your grasp.

PREFACE

You are a creator. You always have been. If you've followed my work and ministry for any amount of time then you know fully well just how much I believe that about you. Seeing as how we're crafted in the image and likeness of God, possessing his characteristics, His attributes, and His essence, it's no secret that, like Him, you and I have been called to create. In the very beginning of it all, long before man and woman were ever placed into the Garden Paradise to enjoy the physical realm, even then there was a burning desire on the part of the Creator to create –

something. That's what creators do, you see. They create. They can't help it.

Authors write. Painters and sculptors create art. Those who have a love of the culinary arts spend their days crafting wonderful foods. We're all creating something – even when we don't realize it and even when we don't feel very creative. Such is the nature of the call of God to co-create. But just as you're called to create the abundant life here within the physical realm of life, you're also attracting certain things according to that same creative power you possess. When I felt the leading of the Holy Spirit driving me to ponder the revelation that's contained within this book, I felt myself asking the question, "What's the difference between attracting and creating?" Is there a difference? If so, what do those differences entail?

You see, day by day, all along the way, you and I are being driven toward greater glories and toward the promise of an abundant life – a life of fulfillment. We're driven to create a life that feels good. As the writer of the Book of James states, every good and perfect thing comes from God. It's no exaggeration to say, then, that what comes from God feels good. By creating the life of God within the realm of earth, you're being driven to create a life that feels good – a life that feels truly satisfying. And along the way, all through the journey of life, there are those moments that sometimes feel anything but good and anything but satisfying. With the joy come also the many moments of sadness and pain – all of those things we wish we never have to experience. And through it all, we're learning and we're growing – we're awakening to the greater, fuller measure of the inner Christ.

The inspiration of this book is a question that I feel must be asked, more now than ever before: "What's the difference between attraction and creation?" Are we here to merely attract into our lives according to our thoughts and beliefs, or are we actually creating something through it all? And, furthermore, do attraction and co-creation work together in some real way? How can we know the difference? When those moments of life come and seem to sweep the rug from underneath our feet, are we attracting those moments into our lives or are we creating those moments? To pose the question in another, more simple way, allow me to ask you, "What role are you playing within your own life?

You've always had a very real role to play. And contrary to the teachings of organized religion, you've also had a very real say in the matters of life, all along – even when it may not have always seemed like it. This is a book that I feel is timely and much-needed. It's needed within the Body of Christ, as we as believers seek to grasp the meaning of the abundant life and recognize the power we've been entrusted with as co-creators with God. It's needed within spirituality because everyone, regardless of religious belief, has a burning desire to create a more satisfying and more meaningful life experience. Above all, it's needed within all of humanity as a tool for awakening. When awakening comes, we not only are able to see more clearly, but with awakening also comes remembrance. We remember who we are

– who we've always been . When we're reminded of who we are, we see that just as He is, so are we.

INTRODUCTION

Since the dawn of humanity, mankind has longed to better understand the mysteries at work within the Universe, pondering not only the true meaning of existence but also the nature of humanity itself. Throughout the ages, many great philosophies have arisen along with countless religions which span the globe – each seeking to in some way better define the meaning of life. Is there some purpose to the many events of life, or are we, as some have suggested, merely left to our own devices and forced to be forever tossed about upon the waves of chance? Even in the beginning of it all, man longed to know and to better understand the role that he had been given to play in the grand scheme of things. "Who am I?" "Why am I here?" "What is the meaning of life itself?" The truth is, there are no simple answers. But answers have always come with awakening, when the mind becomes renewed to spiritual things.

When awakening comes and when the natural, religious mind and its many limitations becomes stripped away and replaced by the limitless nature of Christ, we begin to view life in a much more expansive way than ever before. When awakening comes, in fact, we begin to recognize that we've never been as powerless or as helpless as we sometimes might feel. We begin to realize all the more that we've always had a very real, all-important say in the matters of life, even when it may not have seemed that way. And then, in those moments of recognition and understanding, deep within, there seems to be an internal shift that takes place as hopelessness gives way to hope and as victim-hood gives way to victory. Awakening changes everything.

Regardless of one's faith, one's religious creed or lack thereof, and no matter how he or she chooses to define the things of God, there isn't a person living today who doesn't want a more fulfilling, more abundant life – one filled with contentment and greater satisfaction. Where faith is concerned, isn't that the end-game we've been promised? Didn't Jesus himself extol continuously the promise of an abundant life – a life that could be lived to the fullest? I, for one, refuse to believe that life is meant to be a constant series of struggles, heartaches, and moments of opposition. I refuse to believe that life has to always be difficult and hard to manage. A life of struggle, to me, seems anything but abundant and anything but rewarding.

When I wrote my book *The New Season is Coming*, I shared within a chapter the importance of learning to better understand the many definitions we bring to the moments of life. We're always seeking to in some way define our experiences, as the natural mind grapples to bring definition to literally everything. We know what feels good and we know what feels not as good. For the most part, most individuals, as well-meaning and as sincere as they are, rarely live lives that truly feel good. Is this the abundant life Jesus promised? The question must be asked.

Shouldn't the abundant life feel "good," to some degree, given that every "good" and "perfect" thing has come from God? As we go throughout life, navigating the many, many twists and turns, one thing remains so consistent through it all and that is the role that we're being offered to play in each and every passing moment.

What I've found within my own life and ministry and have seen time and time again throughout more than twenty years of experience in prophetic life coaching sessions is that nothing feels worse and nothing feels more frightening than the feeling of being out of control. When the job is suddenly terminated or when the relationship suddenly ends, it can be devastating, as we're left reeling in the feeling of helplessness. Suffice it to say, all of life is serving to remind us of the role we're being given to play in each and every passing moment of time. And rest assured, we've always been given a very real choice and a very real say in all of those moments – even when it doesn't always feel like it. Feelings can be quite elusive at times and so often misleading – hence, the need for spiritual awakening.

But what role have we been given to play here within the physical world exactly? You're reading this, I would assume, because to some degree you consider yourself a person of faith. Perhaps, like me, you also have a burning, deep desire to better understand the spiritual things. Perhaps, like me, you also have a desire to better understand your own prophetic gifting. If you've found yourself awakened to the greater mysteries of God, renewed within your mind and beginning to question the lies of religion that you once believed, chances are you're now beginning to realize as never before that where life upon Planet Earth is concerned, there's always a certain sense of responsibility involved. Perhaps, by now, you've also started to realize that life within the Kingdom of God requires a certain amount of that same responsibility. Regardless of how faithful you may very well be, you are not and never will be exempted from the role of personal responsibility.

Several weeks ago, during a coaching session, I had a very dear friend and valued client and ministry partner ask if I believe we can call things into being within our lives.

"Absolutely," I replied. The truth is, though, that it doesn't stop there and it isn't really that simple. Though the answer is "Yes," there is much, much more work involved. The global outreach of Identity Network was birthed with the revelation of vision – a revelation that it's always so important to have a vision for the lives we desire to create. After all, the Gospel is "good news." And the good news is that when you dream and imagine the life you desire, if you can see it then you can most certainly have it, as I've always said.

But dreams left within the dream state are simply that – nothing more than dreams. And visions left within the visionary realm are nothing more than visions left to be manifested.

It's not enough to simply dream or to cast vision for your life. Implementation is crucial. It's vital, even. But to move beyond the realm of the dream and the vision, prophetically speaking, comes also the need to better understand the great forces at work behind the scenes in all of Creation. What's working for you? What's working against you? When are the best times to act and to implement strategies? You see, it all matters – every single bit of it. You can claim and speak your promise until even more seasons of your life pass and still see nothing manifest if you don't learn to better discern the creative forces at work around you – and within you. That's the real purpose of this book.

As you join me in the journey into the pages of *Supernatural Attraction and Co-Creation*, I hope that you will begin to not only take stock of your own visions and dreams but that, above all, you would feel inspired as never before to actually, once and for all, finally begin to put those dreams and visions into action. My prayer for you is that you would not only dream of and envision the abundant life you've been promised but that you would begin to manifest it at all cost. My friend, when reading this book, I want you to become so dissatisfied with the complacency and the lies of man-made religion that you would begin to say, "There's gotta be more than this!" There is more. There's much, much more.

What I know to be true is that when we seek, we find. When we knock, doorways are opened. As I've said for years, your level of passion will always be connected to the questions you ask. Jesus himself said that questions are important. Didn't he say, emphatically, that we should ask, seek, and knock? It's time to ask the deeper questions and to look beyond religion. It's time to realize that for far too long, you've been living far beneath your means - and beneath your own creative power. When awakening comes, just as Jesus said, the abundant life can be experienced.

When I wrote *The Universe is at Your Command* and *Creating with Your Thoughts* years ago, I found myself inspired by the Holy Spirit to share with the world a revelation concerning the power of the mind and its many thoughts. The religious mind loves to make excuses, it seems, and will go to any length to keep from taking and accepting personal responsibility. "If it's God's will," it says. "The enemy keeps me from prospering," it laments. "Maybe one day God will bless me, if I just remain faithful," it moans. And time continues to pass. More often than not, the dreams die with the dreamers without ever being fully realized and implemented. Far too often, "One day" never comes, and sincere believers continue to resign themselves to the sidelines of life, being spectators and victims of life rather than being active, conscious, willful participants.

But you can be an exception to religions' many statistics. You, unlike so many others, can not only realize the power of your dreams but can also bring those dreams into the physical, material world. As I've said for years, it's truly not enough to dream and it's never really enough to simply just believe. What are your beliefs creating for you? Have your beliefs created an abundant life? Are you experiencing all that God has for you and can you say that your life is truly satisfying? If not - if those beliefs you hold aren't truly working for you then it's time to not only reassess and analyze those beliefs in a new and different way but it's also time to let some of those old beliefs go. The abundant life and the limitations of the religious, natural mind cannot and do not coexist. As the scriptures remind us, the carnal mind is the very enemy of God and the natural mind cannot even know the things of the Spirit.

But when awakening comes and when the eyes of our understanding become enlightened, as Paul writes, then we begin to realize not only the existence of the more abundant, more fulfilling life we've been offered but we also, in turn, begin to realize the power we've been entrusted with to have exactly what we desire. You, my friend and fellow seeker, have always had the power to accomplish the abundant life. And day after day, not only are you attracting to your life the very things you believe but, in so doing, are also creating the life you now live, according to your faith. This book serves as a testament not only to all who dream of a more abundant, more fulfilling life but, even more so, to any and all who are determined to never settle for just the dream or the vision. This is for those who are determined to create a life of their dreams, even in the here and now. Why are you putting off for "one day" what you've always had the power to have right now?

CHAPTER ONE
SUPERNATURAL ATTRACTION

For as long as man has walked the terrain of the planet called Earth, mankind has longed to better know and to understand the things of the Spirit. Such is the human condition, it seems - a heart that burns with vision. When man and woman were placed into the Garden Paradise, even in the very beginning of it all, even then they couldn't help but dream and to have vision. There were so many adventures to be taken - so many conversations to be had and enjoyed. There were so many mountains to climb and so many beautiful, flowing streams to look upon. What I mean to say, quite simply, is that as long as there has been the ability to think, there has also been the ability to cast vision and the ability to dream. And, for some reason, with those visions and those dreams, always comes a desire for even more.

There's always a desire for more - for greater dreams and for a more far-reaching vision. The mind that envisions having a better-paying job is also the mind that seems to whisper, "Start your own company." The mind that longs for adventure - that so looks forward to the annual vacation - is the same mind that wants financial freedom to be able to travel the entire globe at will. The mind doesn't just want more; it wants much more. And this desire for more, I would suggest even here at the very beginning of our journey together, is, in fact, the very nature of the Godhead now existing bodily. The desire for a more and a greater abundant life is not just mere wishful thinking. Those dreams aren't coming from an overactive imagination. And contrary to popular belief, the desire for more isn't some "enemy" attempting to lure you away into greed. The desire for a more abundant, more prosperous, richer life is the God within you crying out to remind you who you are.

Religion has always had the most uncanny, deadly way of dulling and deafening the inner nature of Christ and causing us to forget the nature of the Godhead dwelling bodily within us.

"Adam," you see, was just as filled with vision as the very Creator who formed and fashioned him from the dust of he ground - who had breathed into him the very Breath of Life which caused the man to become a living, breathing, "thinking" soul. You're aware of the account of Creation, I'm sure - that man was formed in the image and the likeness of God, with the Creator exclaiming, "Let us make man in our image." What you may not be fully aware of, though, is that in that moment of divine, heavenly infusion when man became a living soul he thereby became an extension of God within the physical realm. And like God, man was endued with the ability to get exactly what he wanted. The Creator even remarked as much, expressing that man would have dominion, would be fruitful, and would "multiply."

This multiplication would go far beyond the mere biological ability to reproduce offspring and to bring forth sons and daughters. This blessing of multiplication spoke of something even more heavenly. It spoke of man's own uncanny ability to attract and to create at will, according to his own thoughts and his own visions. In the very beginning, even in the account of Creation, we find that even the Creator had in mind the element of "more." Multiplication, expansion, growth, progression yes, "more" - have always been the nature of the God. And that nature was freely, joyfully imparted into man - the crowing jewel of all
Creation.

In what would become one of my bestselling books, The Universe is at Your Command, I shared an illustration of those first moments of Creation. The illustration, perhaps, offended and boggled the religious minds of some. I shared that long before the worlds were ever formed and long, long before there was ever the physical, human form of man - the "soma" fashioned from he dust of the ground - even then, you and I existed with the Creator. As the stars were hurled onto the tapestry of the night sky, you and I were there, also looking on. You've always been a powerful co-creator with God. Chances are you've simply forgotten that and have begun to feel powerless. The fact is, though, that you and I have never truly been powerless or without hope. The only thing separating you from the life

of your dreams has always been your own religion and the limitations and self-defeating mentality of the carnal, religious mind which has yet to become awakened and renewed to the mind of the inner
Christ.

Here at the very offset of our journey, I share this with you not to humbly suggest but to emphatically state unequivocally that you are as much a creator within the realm of earth as the Creator Himself. There is no distance. There is no separation. There is no "fall" from God's good graces - that is, except within the mind and unless you still believe there to be. Wasn't it interesting, though, that even after the forbidden fruit had been tasted the Creator still came to walk with them in the cool of the day? The "fall" took place not within the heart of God but within the mind of man. And from that fallen mind, came religion with its feelings of sin, of depravity, of self-consciousness rather than God-consciousness, its inferiority complex, its feeling of unworthiness, and an inner voice of victim-hood. When awakening comes, though, and when the mind becomes renewed to the nature of the inner Christ, the soul seems to remember its true identity - remembering that we truly are one with the Godhead and always have been.

You deserve an abundant life. You always have. Your desires for "more" aren't just wishful thinking and it most certainly isn't greedy to want more fulfillment. The very desire to possess the land around you is birthed by the Holy Spirit. In fact, all that you see has already been freely given to you. You already possess the land. As far as the eye can see, wherever the soles of your feet shall trod, it's all already yours. As I've said before, you already have it all!

It's really, truly not enough, though, to have been freely given the abundant life and the promise of a bright, more fulfilling existence; you have to believe it. And for far too long, where most seemingly sincere and well-meaning believers so often miss it is that they fail to see the power of Creation residing within their very own thoughts and beliefs. If you say, "I'll never have the new career," you're absolutely right. And if you say, "I can start my own business," you're also correct. According to the text of the ancient scriptures, as a man thinks, so is he. All throughout the course of human history, mankind has seemed to know, to some degree, the power residing within the mind - even when the illusions of religion have attempted to deafen and to dull the inner, more spiritual senses to the things of God.

What if I were to tell you, here at the very beginning of our journey together, that you're now living the result of the very things you're thinking? Would you find such a claim shocking or outlandish? Would you think such a claim to be heretical and unorthodox? Well, if you do, you shouldn't. After all, even Jesus himself taught and shared as much all throughout his earthly life and ministry. In fact, Jesus had much to say about the powerful,

Kingdom Law of Attraction. Did you know that? It's true. He simply called it "faith."

"And when they came nigh to Jerusalem, unto Bethphage and Bethany, at the mount of Olives, he sendeth forth two of his disciples,

And saith unto them, Go your way into the village over against you: and as soon as ye be entered into it, ye shall find a colt tied, whereon never man sat; loose him, and bring him.

And if any man say unto you, Why do ye this? say ye that the Lord hath need of him; and straightway he will send him hither.

And they went their way, and found the colt tied by the door without in a place where two ways met; and they loose him.

And certain of them that stood there said unto them, What do ye, loosing the colt? And they said unto them even as Jesus had commanded: and they let them go.

And they brought the colt to Jesus, and cast their garments on him; and he sat upon him.

And many spread their garments in the way: and others cut down branches off the trees, and strawed them in the way.

And they that went before, and they that followed, cried, saying, Hosanna; Blessed is he that cometh in the name of the Lord:

Blessed be the kingdom of our father David, that cometh in the name of the Lord: Hosanna in the highest.

And Jesus entered into Jerusalem, and into the temple: and when he had looked round about upon all things, and now the eventide was come, he went out unto Bethany with the twelve.

And on the morrow, when they were come from Bethany, he was hungry:

And seeing a fig tree afar off having leaves, he came, if haply he might find any thing thereon: and when he came to it, he found nothing but leaves; for the time of figs was not yet.

And Jesus answered and said unto it, No man eat fruit of thee hereafter for ever. And his disciples heard it.

And they come to Jerusalem: and Jesus went into the temple, and began to cast out them that sold and bought in the temple, and overthrew the tables of the moneychangers, and the seats of them that sold doves;

And would not suffer that any man should carry any vessel through the temple.

And he taught, saying unto them, Is it not written, My house shall be called of all nations the house of prayer? but ye have made it a den of thieves.

And the scribes and chief priests heard it, and sought how they might destroy him: for they feared him, because all the people was astonished at his doctrine.

And when even was come, he went out of the city.

And in the morning, as they passed by, they saw the fig tree dried up from the roots.

And Peter calling to remembrance saith unto him, Master, behold, the fig tree which thou cursedst is withered away.

And Jesus answering saith unto them, Have faith in God.

For verily I say unto you, That whosoever shall say unto this mountain, Be thou removed, and be thou cast into the sea; and shall not doubt in his heart, but shall believe that those things which he saith shall come to pass; he shall have whatsoever he saith.

Therefore I say unto you, What things soever ye desire, when ye pray, believe that ye receive them, and ye shall have them.

And when ye stand praying, forgive, if ye have ought against any: that your Father also which is in heaven may forgive you your trespasses.

But if ye do not forgive, neither will your Father which is in heaven forgive your trespasses.

And they come again to Jerusalem: and as he was walking in the temple, there come to him the chief priests, and the scribes, and the elders,

And say unto him, By what authority doest thou these things? and who gave thee this authority to do these things? (Mark 11:1-28 KJV)

But what exactly was this power and this authority that Jesus spoke of? What was the authority that caused him to do such things? It was the power of belief - a universal, heavenly principle that had been in place ever since the very beginning, long before the Garden Paradise was ever spoken into existence. It was the Kingdom Law of Attraction - the principle that we will be given exactly what we believe. Such is the very nature of the Godhead. And so it is with our own true natures, as co-creators and as supernaturally attractive souls in the physical realm called life upon Planet Earth.

In sharing with the onlookers the marvelous demonstration, Jesus was sharing, also, the great mystery of the power of belief and of thought. If you do not doubt and simply believe, all things are possible and nothing shall be impossible. We know this to be the case, to some degree, and have been told throughout decades of religion that "all things are possible." But there's more. I've often said for years that religion doesn't truly believe what it claims to believe because if it did then "believers" wouldn't truly be afraid to start the new business, buy the new home, create a more prosperous existence for themselves, and make themselves financially independent. Suffice it to say, if you truly do believe that all things really are possible, then why are continuing to live life as though its filled with so many impossibilities?

What I've seen for years, throughout my own life and ministry and continue to see more and more each day in my coaching sessions with clients, is the single, greatest hindrance to possessing the abundant life is not simply a lack of belief as much as it is a belief in all the wrong things - all those limiting, self-deprecating beliefs that stifle, that numb, and that dull the senses, causing the individuals to feel so unworthy and so, so very powerless. For far too long, you've had "faith;" however, you've had faith in all the wrong things, choosing to view life and all existence through the wrong lens the lens of limitation. We've all been there at one time or another, and this is why it is so important to not only renew the mind but to renew the mind daily, as we experience greater, deeper revelational knowledge of the things of God. The scenery is always changing in the Kingdom, and if you aren't changing and growing and progressing in your beliefs, then you're missing the power which awaits you in the journey.

Are your beliefs working for you? Allow me to ask the question in another way. Does your life feel "good" to you? If not and if the answer is "No," it in no way means that you don't believe. After all, we all believe something. It means that your beliefs have stopped serving you and that you're believing the wrong things - about life, about Creation, about God, and yes, even more so about your very own self and identity. Thankfully, you can change your beliefs. Thankfully, you can always change your mind. You can always replace thoughts with new, awakened, heavenly thoughts. And when you change your thoughts, you change your life. My friend and fellow seeker, it's time to believe again. It's time to stop parroting the religious lies you've been told and indoctrinated to believe. Those visions you have - those dreams of a more abundant, more fulfilling life - have come from God. Contrary to the lies of religion, though, those dreams aren't going to just fulfill themselves. The vision - though it awaits an appointed time and season - isn't going to suddenly just manifest itself on its very own. The abundant life isn't going to just suddenly start "one day."

You have a very real role to play within the creation of your very own life upon Planet Earth. And it's time you begin to view your life in a more heavenly, more transcendent way than ever before - through the lens of the unlimited nature of the Creator within you. As a supernaturally attractive soul and co-creator with God, not only have you been promised an abundant life and not only have you been given the vision for "more," but you've truly been given the very power of all Creation to manifest the life you truly desire and dream of. It's not enough to simply believe or to dream or to cast vision. It's time to bring those dreams into reality in a much more aligned way than ever before by realizing, once and for all, the life you're living right now is a life you've attracted to yourself. And if you aren't satisfied and feeling fully alive, it's time to begin to attract something even "more." As you will see, you do that by realizing the power within our own thoughts.

CHAPTER TWO
PROGRESSION

Throughout the ages, much has been said about the heavenly Law of Attraction. When Rhonda Byrne released her international bestseller *The Secret*, the release became a global phenomenon. Almost overnight, it seemed, the entire globe was swept with a new-found desire to better understand the unseen realm. As never before, it seemed a hunger for spirituality began to sweep the globe in ways we had rarely sen, as even celebrities and politicians began to publicly profess the "secret" of the Law of Attraction. Well, throughout the years I've been honored to have written a few bestselling books of my own, and I can tell you, prophetically speaking, that the power of attraction has never really been a "secret" in the Kingdom of God. At least, it shouldn't be.

As humanity began to question the power of the mind and to wake up to the fact that thoughts really can and do become things, religion, as it always seems to do, contradicted the book and the teachings, labeling it as nothing more than "New Age" fluff. I found myself so excited to see a new-found hunger and passion within humanity for the revelation of attraction; yet, I also found myself dismayed by the childishness of religion. The church, it seems, would much rather debate and argue over semantics and terms and meanings of words than to actually grow up in the things of God. Religion has always worked this way. Rather than seeking after new revelation, new knowledge, and a better, more awakened understanding, the religious mind with it's many, many preconceived notions and ideas always seeks to label and to judge. Religion is not only deafening and dulling to the senses, but religion is actually quite deadly, indeed.

The Universe and all that's within it is progressive. It's expanding. It's always moving and shifting and ever-evolving. Knowledge is the exact same way. Revelation is always growing, as even Creation around us cries out and groans in travail.

Do the scriptures not say that all Creation cries out, waiting in anticipation for the awakening of the sons of God? Even from the very beginning, you see, all Creation has been attempting to get our attention as it continues to reveal to us the matchless glory of a loving Creator. These messages, if we aren't careful, can be overlooked and quickly missed by the eyes blinded by religion's toxic filters. It wasn't all that long ago, really, that many were literally killed - beheaded, burned alive, and stoned to death - for no other reason than that they were free thinkers who questioned the norm.

How did this happen? Where did such oppression begin, particularly where religion is concerned? I share this with you because if you're ever to better underhand the power of attraction within the your own life and also your own ability to co-create with God within the realm of Planet Earth, you're going to have to realize that the only hindrance to your own authority is the religious, natural mind with its many filters of limitation. Why is religion so dangerous? Is it merely because of tradition or orthodoxy? No. Although Jesus himself stated that the traditions of man had made the Word of God to no effect. Beyond the customs, the rituals, and the practices of even the most sincere religions of the world, lies the most damning, most deadly concept of all - the illusion of separation.

Throughout the ages, so much knowledge and truth has been judged as "heresy" by the church, and many have been persecuted and even killed because of it. There was a time, not all that long ago, when many believed Earth to be flat. There was a time when many believed the Earth to be the center of the Universe.

But, still, through it all, knowledge has always increased as, little by little within each passing generation, humanity has continued to ask questions. All of Creation is progressive and moving forward. So much of what religion has termed "New Age," in fact, is actually the truth of the Kingdom. Religion has always had an uncanny way of playing to our fears by promoting judgment and keeping humanity from asking questions. But truth and revelation have always continued to evolve and to expand and the "knowledge" of the glory of the LORD has continued to cover the Earth as the waters cover the seas.

I want you to be so hungry for the things of God that you continue to ask questions - that you continue to question the conventional wisdom of the day and the religious norm. Today, as never before, advancements in science and in the medical arts are being made daily. Scientific breakthroughs are being made more rapidly than ever before. Today, there is a togetherness that didn't exist even decades ago as, with a click of a button, we're able to connect with almost anyone on Planet Earth thanks to the world wide web. When Jesus walked about doing good and healing all that were oppressed of the devil, there were no such advancements. Words, terminology, and labels were much different. Yet, even then, mysteriously, there seemed to be some understanding of the great forces at work within Creation - even as the Pharisees and the many onlookers asked by what "authority" Jesus performed his many marvelous feats.

Even then, all those centuries ago, Jesus spoke of the power of the mind and of the power residing within the thoughts we think. As the scriptures remind us, as a man thinketh in his heart, so is he. I wanted to include this chapter to say, even here at the very beginning of our journey together, that it's the will of God for you to become so consumed with hunger for the things of the Spirit that you never dare to stop questioning and pursuing the more heavenly things - in spite of what organized religion may say. What I've seen throughout my own years of teaching the Law of Attraction is that, regardless of labels and regardless of the terminology we use, humanity is beginning to awaken as never before to the revelation of Kingdom attraction as men and women, young and old, are starting to realize that we are creating life according to our thoughts and beliefs. And though Jesus never used the term "Law of Attraction," he spoke emphatically, continuously, about the power of belief, sharing that we can have an abundant life and that we will be given exactly what we believe. Yes, the "secret" really is nothing new at all.

The element of "more" has always been so deeply interwoven into the fabric of Creation that literally every generation that has ever walked upon Planet Earth has in some way felt the effects of it. With every passing dream, every vision, and, yes, even with every question posed as believers have continued to ask, seek, and knock, the "knowledge" of the glory of the LORD has grown and continued to increase, no matter the time or the season. It was the Prophet Haggai who said the glory of the latter house would be greater than the former. And, interestingly enough, we find the analogy used even within the Book of Job, as the writer makes mention of progression and forward expansion. *"Though thy beginning was small, yet thy latter end should greatly increase." (Job 8:7 KJV)* All throughout time, there has always been the element of increase - the element of "more" - interwoven into all Creation around us as even Creation itself has travailed to bring about awakening.

Throughout the ages, even when religion sought to silence those who sought to uncover the great mysteries regarding the power of thoughts, the Spirit continued to inspire, continued to give dreams and visions, and continued even to share new insight and new revelation.

As the political elements of religion began to give rise to an allegiance with the Roman Empire in the first few centuries of the church, rather than continuing in the faith once delivered to the saints, there arose mighty political forces within the church who sought to silence all who would question it. Yet the heavenly, cosmic laws in operation within Creation never ceased. And the same power and authority that had been given to Adam in the Garden Paradise in the very beginning continued to reside within humanity. Though seemingly buried and forgotten, the authority to create and to attract was just as much the birthright of man as it had ever been. And as knowledge of the things of God continued to expand and to progress, little by little, awakening continued to come, as the eyes of understanding began to become enlightened.

You may be wondering why I chose to include this chapter, detailing the early history of the church. What does such religious opposition have to do with the power of attraction and the heavenly force of Creation residing within us? The answer is absolutely everything. When was the last time you heard a fellow believer say, "You shouldn't study the Law of Attraction because it's not in the Bible?" When was the last time you heard a believer, though sincere and very well-meaning in their faith, exclaim, "If it's the will of God, I'll have more." "If it's God's will, I'll have a better job." I'll be financially independent if God wants me to be blessed." On and on it goes, really. And time continues to pass as dreams and visions continue to be taken to the grave, along with those who once dreamed and envisioned them. My friend, time is not a luxury that you have. It's time to look beyond religion and begin to see the truth of the Gospel - the true Gospel of the Kingdom, which has absolutely nothing to do with a global religion seeking to keep you in mental, emotional, and spiritual bondage.

It wasn't all that long ago that I found myself entangled within my own limitations within my own mind. Before there was ever an Identity Network and before there were ever bestselling books being published across the globe, I, too, was a believer who constantly said, "If it be God's will." "Maybe I can be successful one day," I thought. "Maybe, if God chooses, I can be financially prosperous." "Maybe one day God will allow me to write a book or two," I thought.

But the books didn't write themselves. Identity Network didn't just suddenly, mysteriously become imparted to me from on-high. And, above all, the Gospel didn't just begin to miraculously take itself around the world. No. There was a role to play - a role that I had been given to play within my own life. I awakened to the power of Creation residing within me when I realized that the realm of the Spirit far surpasses and far supersedes the realm of man-made religion. I hope and pray the same for you, even now as you read these words. It's not enough to read the Bible, and, in fact, it's really not even enough to "just believe." You need to know what you believe, why you believe it, and, if something is not working you need to allow yourself the freedom to change those beliefs.

The truth of the matter is that there are beliefs you're hold on to that should have been put to death a long, long time ago. As the Apostle Paul write, there are "childish things" that you should have stopped to believing in long, long ago. To come into the maturity of the faith demands that we begin to look beyond the lies of religion. Awakening begins when this happens - when we realize that there has always, always been much, much "more" and that the "more" of God has always been our birthright. When you begin to realize who you are - who you truly are - and what you truly deserve, you begin to awaken to the nature of Christ. Then and only then will you begin to realize that there's never been any separation at all - except within your own mind. Some would ask, "Why is it important that I better understand the power of attraction and the power of co-creating with God?" In truth, in short, it's because it is the Gospel of the Kingdom, and there can be no true abundant life without one's own awakening to that revelation.

Day after day, moment by moment, somewhere in the world, there is a gospel going forth - but it isn't the Gospel. Somewhere there are believers huddled in masses around an altar, sincerely crying out for revival, shouting, "God, give me an abundant life!" But, for most, abundance never truly comes. Although the soul prospers, most never truly experience the prosperity of a truly rich and abundance life while in the natural, physical realm of Planet Earth. This is not the promise you've been given. This is not the message of the Kingdom. Those dreams and those visions have always served a very real purpose, and that purpose has always been to awaken you to the truth of who you are - to the truth of who you've always been all along.

And so, in closing this chapter and in preparing you for our journey together into the ancient mysteries of the Kingdom - the mysteries having been revealed in the power of Christ my hope is that you would begin to ask the deeper, more heavenly questions. My friend and fellow seeker, the truth of the matter is that this is not all there is. There is always more. There is always greater revelation - greater abundance. There is always, always more where life within the Kingdom of Heaven is concerned. It's time to see God while in the land of the living - not waiting for some future, distant time or place. As I shared within my book *How Does God Speak?* All of Heaven has permeated and invaded all of the realm of physical humanity and all Creation is crying out in an attempt to remind humanity of the sonship - of the attractive, co-creative power - it possesses.

Today, as never before, humanity is beginning to awaken and in this generation, as advancements are continuing to be made in the sciences, confirmation after confirmation continue to arise, reminding us that there is truly a great and expansive force at work where the mind is concerned. And so what are we as believers to make of this? Are we to simply say, "That's 'New Age' and has no place within the church?" Or are we, instead, to begin to ask, to seek, and to knock, as Jesus said, and begin to move into maturity in the Body of Christ, beginning to see and to realize that we've been given power within this physical realm? The choice, as with all things, is entirely our own.

Change is never easy and it's always uncomfortable. It hurts for a moment to realize that we've been wrong about so much.

However, nothing is more painful than a wasted life - a life spend waiting, wishing, and hoping for the things of God without ever truly seeing the fruits of our labor. As the scriptures have said, the harvest is plentiful and yet the laborers are very few. It's time to begin to realize that just as Creation is expanding, a need for greater knowledge and understanding where the things of God are concerned is paramount.

The Law of Attraction is not only real and is not only a bedrock principle within the Kingdom of God where the pursuit of the abundant life is concerned but it is, as you will soon see, a very integral part of the Gospel itself. Not only will you be given what you believe but you will be given exactly what you believe, just as Jesus promised. And for far too long, you've believed the wrong things about life, about Creation, about God, and, above all, about your very own self. You've always had more power in all matters of daily life than you've ever realized and much greater power than you've truly ever given yourself credit for. As we journey into this book, into the "more" of the Kingdom, I want your faith to rise as never before so that you would become awakened within your mind to the powers residing not only all around you but, above all, within you. After all, as Jesus said, the Kingdom of Heaven is within you. There is no separation, except where the unawakened mind is concerned. The mind which has yet to be renewed and awakened to the limitlessness of Christ is the only barrier - the only impediment - to the abundant life. And, as you will soon see as we journey together into the greater truths of the mysteries of attraction and co-creation in the Kingdom of God, there has always been very "good news" in existence for us all. The Gospel is still good news. And the good news is that you and I have never been without hope.

CHAPTER THREE
THAT WHICH WAS LOST

"*And Jesus entered and passed through Jericho.*

And, behold, there was a man named Zacchaeus, which was the chief among the publicans, and he was rich.

And he sought to see Jesus who he was; and could not for the press, because he was little of stature.

he ran before, and climbed up into a sycomore tree to see him: for he was to pass that way.

And when Jesus came to the place, he looked up, and saw him, and said unto him, Zacchaeus, make haste, and come down; for to day I must abide at thy house.

And he made haste, and came down, and received him joyfully.

And when they saw it, they all murmured, saying, That he was gone to be guest with a man that is a sinner.

And Zacchaeus stood, and said unto the Lord: Behold, Lord, the half of my goods I give to the poor; and if I have taken any thing from any man by false accusation, I restore him fourfold.

Jesus said unto him, This day is salvation come to this house, forsomuch as he also is a son of Abraham.

For the Son of man is come to seek and to save that which was lost.

And as they heard these things, he added and spake a parable, because he was nigh to Jerusalem, and because they thought that the kingdom of God should immediately appear.

He said therefore, A certain nobleman went into a far country to receive for himself a kingdom, and to return.

And he called his ten servants, and delivered them ten pounds, and said unto them, Occupy till I come.

But his citizens hated him, and sent a message after him, saying, We will not have this man to reign over us.

it came to pass, that when he was returned, having received the kingdom, then he

commanded these servants to be called unto him, to whom he had given the money, that he might know how much every man had gained by trading.

Then came the first, saying, Lord, thy pound hath gained ten pounds.

And he said unto him, Well, thou good servant: because thou hast been faithful in a very little, have thou authority over ten cities.

And the second came, saying, Lord, thy pound hath gained five pounds.

And he said likewise to him, Be thou also over five cities.

And another came, saying, Lord, behold, here is thy pound, which I have kept laid up in a napkin:

For I feared thee, because thou art an austere man: thou takest up that thou layedst not down, and reapest that thou didst not sow.

And he saith unto him, Out of thine own mouth will I judge thee, thou wicked servant. Thou knewest that I was an austere man, taking up that I laid not down, and reaping that I did not sow:

Wherefore then gavest not thou my money into the bank, that at my coming I might have required mine own with usury?

And he said unto them that stood by, Take from him the pound, and give it to him that hath ten pounds.

(And they said unto him, Lord, he hath ten pounds.)

For I say unto you, That unto every one which hath shall be given; and from him that hath not, even that he hath shall be taken away from him." (Luke 19:1-26 KJV)

In the above referenced text, we find an illustration not only of the Gospel message but also of the power of attraction itself. Whether you've ever taken the time to realize it or not, you are your very own self-fulfilling prophecy and you always have been. There's never been a time in your life when you haven't gotten "more" of the same, according to your beliefs. You see, not only has Creation always been progressive in nature - continuously expanding and progressing forward - but you and I, with the power of our own beliefs, are always continuously manifesting even more of what we believe. The beliefs you hold, they will expand. They will grow. They will continue to produce in like manner. And as Jesus said, every one who has will be given even "more" and those who have not, even what they have will be taken away. You're always going to reproduce in your life according to the beliefs you hold and according to the thoughts you think.

It didn't begin with the words of Jesus, though, as he walked upon Planet Earth and taught concerning the things of the Kingdom. Though he came to share a message of "good news" - a very real, very heavenly and most powerful "Gospel." Even as God looked onto the empty nothingness that existed before He ever uttered the words "Let there be," even then, there were cosmic and heavenly laws in full operation: The Law of Attraction and The Law of Creation. Even then, before the words were ever uttered the words which would yield and bring forth the manifestation of all existence - there was a principle in effect which would bring to pass every vision and every thought. It's no exaggeration really to say that long before God ever spoke, God first thought. Before God spoke, God envisioned. The images of His Creation were already residing within the Divine Mind long before He ever uttered a single word. And He believed without doubt that His words would come to pass and would manifest. I've always found it rather remarkable the words of Jesus in the above referenced passage taken from the synoptic Gospel of John. Isn't it rather interesting the mention of seeking and saving that which had been lost being made within the same context of stewardship - of tending to responsibly to what one has been given? It's no coincidence, I assure you. It was one stream of thought, as Jesus spoke. And he spoke of stewardship because, to an infinite degree, stewardship is in perfect alignment with the message of the Gospel of the Kingdom Jesus taught. He came to seek and to save that which had been lost. And to better understand the immense and enormous power residing within you, you must first begin to understand the context of the Gospel itself.

It's often misquoted. It's often been misaligned - often even unintentionally. This is why it's vastly important that we study to show ourselves approved and not simply take someone's words for the matter. Notice, contrary to the teachings of religion, Jesus never said that he had come to seek and to save "them" that were lost. Although some translations convey this meaning, the original text, in Aramaic, notes a specific, very singular "that," rather than a collective "them." Yes, the Son of Man had come with a very divine and heavenly mandate upon his life. Jesus had come with a very real, very transcendent mission to accomplish. And it was for this cause that the Son of

God was made manifested, according to the epistle of John.

But what exactly was "that?" What exactly had he come to seek and to save? What was the one singular thing? Sure, religion, as always, would love nothing more than to depict some cosmic power play between daylight and the darkness between the forces of good and the forces of evil - as if the "enemy" truly has such power. He doesn't and never has. Religion would love nothing more than to remind you that you're a depraved, fallen sinner, somehow separated from God's good graces all because a man and woman ages ago ate of the forbidden fruit. Again, with all respect, it's time to put away childish things and to once and for all do away with the fairy tales. There was no tree of "good" and "evil." It didn't exist. There was only a tree of the "knowledge" of good and evil.

And when the fruit of the tree of the "knowledge" of good and evil had been partaken of, then there came a consciousness of sin which separated man from God within his own mind - and the man and the woman hid in shame for fear and guilt.

As I've said for years, there was a very real, very cataclysmic fall that did take place. However, it's not as religion suggests. And never once have you and I ever been separated from the mercy and the good graces of a loving Creator. The fall took place within the mind of man and never within the heart of God. When the "knowledge" of good and evil came to man, a cloud came over his unlimited mind, blinding him to the things of his eternal "I AM-ness." In an instant, when the consciousness of God became overtaken by a consciousness of sin and of judgment, there seemed to come such a deep, otherworldly mental fog. There came such an intense forgetfulness. In an instant, it was as if man had suddenly, shockingly forgotten how unlimited his power truly was.

He forgot that he had been created and crafted in the very image and in the very likeness of God. Though he been had formed and fashioned form the dust of the ground, within him resided a very real treasure - the Breath of Life. It was the same Breath of Life that had spoken into existence the entirety of the cosmos only a matter of days before. There truly is, as the Apostle Paul so eloquently and poetically wrote, a treasure within "earthen vessels." There is an "excellency of the power." Yet, in a moment of forgetfulness, rather than viewing his true nature as that of the glory of God - the treasure within - man began to view himself as nothing more than dirty, mired clay. And for centuries, religion has continued to remind humanity, "You're nothing more than dirt." But that's not the Gospel. And suffice it to say, that doesn't seem to be very good news.

In what would become the greatest game of hide and seek ever played, man would for countless centuries come to feel isolated and so separated from the Creator. He would view himself as nothing more than a sinner in need of redemption. In fact, he would feel so very separated and so very distanced from the nature of God that he would create many various religions as a means to find good favor with the the Creator once again. It always seemed so very futile, though. Man would still dream and would still possess heavenly vision. Deep within, deep at his very core, even while hiding, man seemed to always yearn for "more." Somewhere deep within, beneath the religious mind, somewhere deep down, there had always existed an inner voice which whispered,

"There's more than this. I am more than this." And time continued to pass and dreams continued to be dreamed but never fulfilled.

And then, in the fullness of time, Jesus came thankfully. He went about doing good and healing all that were oppressed of the devil. God was with him, according to the Book of Acts. And through it all, there was only one message truly ever shared - the message of the Kingdom. But what did it all mean?

Through it all, Jesus attempted to remind man of "that" which had been lost - of "that" which had been forgotten. He spoke of the Kingdom of God often in cryptic, seemingly veiled ways - often even in code, it seemed. To the religious elite of the day, the words seemed meaningless. But to them that had "an ear to hear," awakening would come. And when the Pharisees and the religious elite asked Jesus by what "authority" he performed his miraculous deeds, in his own unique way, he attempted to remind even them that they had always possessed the same divine authority also, although they had forgotten all about it - although their religious traditions had blinded their eyes.

The Gospel has always been a message of remembrance. It has always been the means by which man is asked lovingly to remember who he truly is and has always been. The message Jesus shared was one of remembrance in that it continuously, often in cryptic ways, pointed to the true, inner nature of man - "The Kingdom of Heaven is within you." The message was one of belief and one which always sought to direct the attention of the believers inward, rather than outward. While the Pharisees and the religious elite of the day sought to always look externally, Jesus spoke of the hidden, buried "treasure" being "hidden" in a field - the treasure within the earthen vessels mentioned by the Apostle Paul. But the message was also one of growth, of progression, and of expansiveness - one of being born again. Interestingly, within the original language of the text, to be born again quite literally means to be born and reborn continuously, over and over and over again. The message of the Kingdom - the Gospel - has always been one of transformation from within.

By what power and what "authority" did Jesus perform his many notable works? In short, by the same authority that even the Pharisees and the religious elite possessed within themselves. Even they possessed the power to become transformed, according to their thoughts and beliefs. *"These words spake Jesus, and lifted up his eyes to heaven, and said, Father, the hour is come; glorify thy Son, that thy Son also may glorify thee:*

As thou hast given him power over all flesh, that he should give eternal life to as many as thou hast given him.

And this is life eternal, that they might know thee the only true God, and Jesus Christ, whom thou hast sent.

I have glorified thee on the earth: I have finished the work which thou gavest me to do.

And now, O Father, glorify thou me with thine own self with the glory which I had with thee before the world was.

I have manifested thy name unto the men which thou gavest me out of the world: thine they were, and thou gavest them me; and they have kept thy word.

Now they have known that all things whatsoever thou hast given me are of thee.

For I have given unto them the words which thou gavest me; and they have received them, and have known surely that I came out from thee, and they have believed that thou didst send me.

I pray for them: I pray not for the world, but for them which thou hast given me; for they are thine.

And all mine are thine, and thine are mine; and I am glorified in them.

And now I am no more in the world, but these are in the world, and I come to thee. Holy Father, keep through thine own name those whom thou hast given me, that they may be one, as we are.

While I was with them in the world, I kept them in thy name: those that thou gavest me I have kept, and none of them is lost, but the son of perdition; that the scripture might be fulfilled.

And now come I to thee; and these things I speak in the world, that they might have my joy fulfilled in themselves.

14 I have given them thy word; and the world hath hated them, because they are not of the world, even as I am not of the world.

I pray not that thou shouldest take them out of the world, but that thou shouldest keep them from the evil.

They are not of the world, even as I am not of the world.

Sanctify them through thy truth: thy word is truth.

As thou hast sent me into the world, even so have I also sent them into the world.

And for their sakes I sanctify myself, that they also might be sanctified through the truth.

Neither pray I for these alone, but for them also which shall believe on me through their word;

That they all may be one; as thou, Father, art in me, and I in thee, that they also may be one in us: that the world may believe that thou hast sent me.

And the glory which thou gavest me I have given them; that they may be one, even as we are one:

I in them, and thou in me, that they may be made perfect in one; and that the world may know that thou hast sent me, and hast loved them, as thou hast loved me.

Father, I will that they also, whom thou hast given me, be with me where I am; that they may behold my glory, which thou hast given me: for thou lovedst me before the foundation of the world.

O righteous Father, the world hath not known thee: but I have known thee, and these have known that thou hast sent me. And I have declared unto them thy name, and will declare it: that the love wherewith thou hast loved me may be in them, and I in them. (John 17:1-26 KJV)

Within the prayer of Jesus, we find what is perhaps the single greatest reference to the "that" which he had come to seek and to save. The words of Jesus offer to us a glimpse into what had been "lost." It was, in fact, man's own ability to recognize the glorious, creative, attractive power he had always possessed - even from the very beginning. You see, there has always been oneness - total and complete divine union within the Godhead. Never has there truly been a moment of separation between man and God - except within the mind of man. The glory of creative power has always existed within humanity, and it has never been taken away. The Gospel and the "good news" is that the same power which raised Jesus to life again is the same power which has always, always existed within humanity. Contrary to what the religious pundits continue to exclaim, you truly are created in the image and in the likeness of God, and like Him, you are called to create. The same power which formed the worlds and created the cosmos in the very beginning is the exact same power which now resides within you and is the power through which you and I create our lives and the entire world around us.

CHAPTER FOUR
AS A MAN THINKETH

When you change your thoughts, you change your life. This statement is by far one of my most quotes phrases and, to some degree, sums up the very mission of Identity Network around the world. When the Holy Spirit first birthed within me the vision to take the Gospel around the world all those years ago and when I first became aware of my own prophetic gifting, what I began to realize more and more was that although the abundant life has been promised, few rarely ever attain it while in the land of the living. My Friend, it's truly not enough to believe in the existence of an abundant life, and it's truly not enough to believe that Jesus came to offer life and offer it more abundantly; that life must be lived. It's time to not only claim your divine and heavenly promise but begin to realize also that you have a very real and very important role to play in bringing about your very own abundance.

"As a man thinketh in his heart, so is he," according to the ancient text of the scriptures. This passage of text not only implies the great, creative power residing within humanity but emphatically, directly states that power resides within the realm of thought. In order to better understand the truth regarding the universal Law of Attraction as well as the Law of Creation, it's imperative that one understands the realm of thought. What you are thinking not only is directing the course of your day but it is directly contributing to the overall outcome of your life. When I was awakened years ago to the power of thought forms, I began to realize more and more the role I'd been given to play within the outcome of my very own life. As a fellow believer and seeker, you believe God; however, you always believe certain things about yourself and you always have. Those thoughts have always manifested and continue to, even as you read these words.

Even thought forms are progressive in nature, bringing about even "more" of what we focus upon, but you don't have to take my word for it. Just think for a moment. When was the last time you found yourself beginning your day in rush hour traffic during your morning commute on your way to work when you found yourself overcome with anger and a bout of rag? When the other driver cut ahead of you in traffic, I would imagine that you had a few choice words.

And even if you never even uttered a sound, in the moment I can almost guarantee that you had a few choice thoughts. And how was the rest of your day after that? Think back for a moment. Chances are, even after arriving at work it seemed as though nothing ever went right. The computers were slow. Your coworkers seemed to have the worst attitudes that day. That was also the day your boss asked you to stay late and all throughout the day it seemed as though you just never could get ahead. It was a bad day. And then you took that bad day home with you and had that argument with your significant other. Even the kids seemed so irritating that day.

Thoughts not only become things but thoughts direct the outcome of the day and also, as a result, the outcome of life itself. It simply cannot be said enough that thoughts become things and that thoughts, regardless of their nature, continue to build and to grow and to expand. Where the mind goes, all the energy of your life will follow. Yes; you've always been directing your thoughts in some way or another - even when you may not have been aware of it. It's truly to exaggeration to say that where the mind goes, literally, all of your days will follow.

In sharing the revelation of the Law of Attraction and the Law of Creation, I felt inspired by the Holy Spirit to include this chapter as a way to inspire you to become much more aware of the power you've always possessed. Remember, you're the very image of God within the realm of earth. You're a Creator, and just as He is, so are you in this present world. Creators, by their very nature, create. They can't help it. Writers write. Painters pain. Creators of all sorts, create by their very natures.

Today, chances are as you look to your own life and to your very own existence upon Planet Earth you find yourself feeling not only dissatisfied but the element of abundance perhaps seems far-off and very distant. What I find more and more throughout many prophetic coaching sessions is that, in truth, most people not only fail to love their lives but, for the most part, they rarely even like their lives. Life, for most, just doesn't feel good. It feels bad.

We know, according to the scriptures that every good and perfect thing comes from above - from God - with whom there is no variation or shadow of turning. In other words, that which is "good" is from God, simply put. I, for one, refuse to believe that life is meant to be a series of constant battles and constant, daily struggles. That life seems anything but abundant, and it seems anything but "good." In this world there will be times of testing and times of tribulation, just as Jesus said. However, life doesn't have to always be bad, and it most certainly, most assuredly doesn't have to always feel like a constant, never ending struggle. Where religion has so often failed humanity is it has always seemed to present the abundant life in some distant, some futuristic and otherworldly and spiritual way. Part of beginning to fully embrace the goodness of the abundant life you've been promised is to begin to realize that the abundant life is a present reality for the here and now - that is, if you can see it and choose to believe it.

Heaven has never been reserved solely for some future, distant place and time. Heaven has always been in the here and now, as a present reality because it's always been within you. Whether you've ever taken the time to realize it or not, you've always been an active, willing participant in the outcome of your own life even when it may have seemed that you were nothing more than a sideline spectator. Even those who resign themselves to the sidelines are still very much in the game of life, always contributing to the outcome of every moment with the thoughts they think. As far as the Kingdom of Heaven is concerned, the truth is that no one is ever exempt from the role of personal responsibility; no one is ever immune from the creative power of their very own thoughts. What you think, you ultimately are.

When Rebekah came to me not long ago, asking for a prophetic Word form the LORD, it was immediately obvious to me that she was not only dissatisfied with how thing were going but it was obvious to me that, for her, life didn't feel good. Perhaps as you now find yourself reading these words, you feel the same about your own life. We've all been there. For most, the feeling of discontentment and dissatisfaction stems from the feeling of helplessness. Helplessness, for most, so often leads to hopelessness. But, thankfully, as the scriptures remind us, we are not as those who have no hope.

Rebekah is one of many, many thousands of individuals whose life was transformed the moment she realized that everything around her hinged entirely upon her own thoughts. Like so many countless other individuals, Rebekah realized that she could begin her own business, write her own book, gain her own financial freedom, and create the life of her dreams. You see, there are those who wait on God without ever taking a step of faith and then there are those who, while they're waiting, begin to actually do for themselves what they've been called to do. The Law of Attraction is equally as practical as it is spiritual and heavenly. Because Heaven has always been within and because the power to create has always existed within our very own beliefs and thoughts, we've never had to wait for some distant, future, far-off time to experience the Kingdom of Heaven.

Your life, as you will see, is the result of what you're choosing to think. And, as with all things, you do have a choice to make even where your thought life is concerned. It's not enough to simply envision a more rich and fulfilling life - the life of abundance that Jesus spoke of - what you think about your life matters, and it's time you become more aware of your thoughts than ever before if you're ever going to truly harness the immense power of Creation you've been given. When awakening comes, you begin to see that Heaven has never truly been all that far away. In fact, it's just as close as your very next breath and even more natural.

And so, what exactly do our thoughts have to do with the power of attraction and creation and, even more importantly, what do those thoughts mean where the journey of faith is concerned? Some have asked how, exactly, does the heavenly Law of Attraction truly tie to the Gospel of the Kingdom. In order to better understand, it's crucial that you recognize once and for all who you truly are - who you've always been. You are not simply a sinner saved by grace - merely some depraved and fallen specimen, destined to forever seek after God's good graces. No. You are as much a powerful Creator as the Creator Himself, and you always have been.

You have the mind of Christ. That heavenly mind, my friend and fellow seeker, isn't something that you're seeking after in hopes of attaining, and it isn't something that one day, suddenly, will magically and divinely be imparted into you. No. It's a present reality. You have the mind of Christ. The issue, though, is that you haven't always allowed it to work for you. Rather than viewing the natural world around you from the lens of the Spirit, you've chosen for most of your life, instead, to view the natural world in a very natural way - with natural sight. And as a result, you've created even more of the same with very little change. Allow me to explain.

When the Apostle Paul spoke of the importance of having the mind renewed, he didn't speak of some future, distant time or place. Instead, he spoke of the mind of Christ being a very present and even a very tangible reality. The great mysteries of the ages, in fact, can be summed up in the single theme of the Christ in you. Do you desire hope? Most of all, do you desire more?" Well, the desire itself is proof positive that even now there is the Christ in you. Your purpose and your mission, is to simply allow it to be.

The lens through which you choose to view life will directly determine the outcome of your life, as I've always said. And for far too long, you've been looking at life through the wrong filters - through the wrong lens. Allow me to say it to you another way. You've been looking at life through the wrong mindset, with all the wrong thoughts! This can be changed the moment you begin to recognize your own creative, heavenly power residing within your own thoughts. The Kingdom authority you've always heard about is very real, and it's tied directly to your very own thoughts and beliefs.

"If there be therefore any consolation in Christ, if any comfort of love, if any fellowship of the Spirit, if any bowels and mercies,

Fulfil ye my joy, that ye be likeminded, having the same love, being of one accord, of one mind.

Let nothing be done through strife or vainglory; but in lowliness of mind let each esteem other better than themselves.

Look not every man on his own things, but every man also on the things of others.

Let this mind be in you, which was also in Christ Jesus:

Who, being in the form of God, thought it not robbery to be equal with God:

But made himself of no reputation, and took upon him the form of a servant, and was made in the likeness of men:

And being found in fashion as a man, he humbled himself, and became obedient unto death, even the death of the cross.

Wherefore God also hath highly exalted him, and given him a name which is above every name:

That at the name of Jesus every knee should bow, of things in heaven, and things in earth, and things under the earth;

And that every tongue should confess that Jesus Christ is Lord, to the glory of God the Father.

Wherefore, my beloved, as ye have always obeyed, not as in my presence only, but now much more in my absence, work out your own salvation with fear and trembling.

For it is God which worketh in you both to will and to do of his good pleasure.

Do all things without murmurings and disputings:

That ye may be blameless and harmless, the sons of God, without rebuke, in the midst of a crooked and perverse nation, among whom ye shine as lights in the world;

Holding forth the word of life; that I may rejoice in the day of Christ, that I have not run in vain, neither laboured in vain.

Yea, and if I be offered upon the sacrifice and service of your faith, I joy, and rejoice with you all.

For the same cause also do ye joy, and rejoice with me.

But I trust in the Lord Jesus to send Timotheus shortly unto you, that I also may be of good comfort, when I know your state.

For I have no man likeminded, who will naturally care for your state.

For all seek their own, not the things which are Jesus Christ's.

But ye know the proof of him, that, as a son with the father, he hath served with me in the gospel.

Him therefore I hope to send presently, so soon as I shall see how it will go with me.

But I trust in the Lord that I also myself shall come shortly.

Yet I supposed it necessary to send to you Epaphroditus, my brother, and companion in labour, and fellowsoldier, but your messenger, and he that ministered to my wants.

For he longed after you all, and was full of heaviness, because that ye had heard that he had been sick.

For indeed he was sick nigh unto death: but God had mercy on him; and not on him only, but on me also, lest I should have sorrow upon sorrow.

I sent him therefore the more carefully, that, when ye see him again, ye may rejoice, and that I may be the less sorrowful.

Receive him therefore in the Lord with all gladness; and hold such in reputation:

Because for the work of Christ he was nigh unto death, not regarding his life, to supply your lack of service toward me." (Philippians 2:1-30 KJV)

Within the spiritual teachings of the Apostle Paul in his epistle to the early church, we find that not only did the early church believe the mind of Christ to be a very real, very present reality but we also find that it believed wholeheartedly that creative power is triggered entirely by belief. Yes; even as you read these words, the mind of Christ - the Divine Mind which was so influential in orchestrating and enacting the moment of Creation in the very beginning - is alive and well within you. This mind is your truest and most sincere nature. But to begin to better understand the power you truly possess, you're going to have to let it be.

Creative power is within you, according to your thoughts and beliefs. Recognize it.

CHAPTER FIVE
WHAT'S IN A NAME?

As we journey together into the ancient, greater mysteries surrounding the Kingdom Laws of Attraction and Creation, my prayer for you is that you would recognize that you are both a heavenly attractive soul as well as a divine, sovereign creator, just as the Creator Himself. After all, is it not written in the scriptures and didn't Jesus himself even make mention of the fact that we are all gods? To the natural, religiousmind, such a claim seems so blasphemous - like such heresy, in fact.

It was the same even then as the religious elite of the day sought to stone Jesus for his message of the Kingdom. Religion would always much rather look to the sky to find Heaven rather than look within. Jesus was crucified for such shocking claims.

But, as a god - as a powerful attractive soul and creator - you've been vested with not only power and authority within the realm of physicality known as life upon Planet Earth but you've also been given certain unalienable rights where your true nature is concerned. And as we journey together into the truth regarding those rights and that authority, it's time that you begin to realize as never before that not only are you creating and crafting the outcome of your life but that your thoughts are part of a much larger, more vast, intricately connected force within Creation itself. Your thoughts matter not only in that they are important but they matter, literally speaking, in that they are constantly materializing - the realm of thought materializes into the realm of physicality.

As of the time of this writing, the world is not what it once was. As I write these words we now face a pandemic as sickness spans the globe and as fear continues to rise. Writing these words to you, I would be remiss if I didn't say that right now we're facing the pandemic of COVID-19, and fear of "Coronavirus" is at an all-time high all throughout the world. There's something about words and definitions that bring such power. There's truly something about a "name." No matter where you are in the world, as of the time of this writing, somehow you're now experiencing the far-reaching effects of this global scare. Businesses are closing. Supplies are quickly being taken from shelves, as everyone seems to want to prepare for the worst. In no exaggeration, this seems to be an unprecedented time in the world.

I make mention of this within this book for two reasons. First, I want to be very honest and transparent with you that although we have immense power within the natural realm according to our thoughts and beliefs, there are those moments when even the strongest among us can face uncertainty and unfamiliarity. No one is exempt from the moments of tribulation that comes to the world, just as Jesus said. Secondly, more importantly, I make mention of this because it seems so fitting. I would be remiss if I did not use a very real, very practical example of everyday life when speaking of the power of Attraction and of the heavenly Law of Creation. Names bring with them such meaning.

Thinking of this global pandemic, I find myself reminded of the words of Job when he said the very thing that he feared most had come upon him. And I find myself questioning what such a statement within the holy scriptures might mean where the Law of Attraction is concerned. Names have meaning and bring with them so much weight, in that when we hear certain words, our minds naturally bring connotation and visualization. Visualization, in fact - those inner, mental images - are the catalysts of the Law of Attraction. I cannot help but ask, what comes to mind when you hear the name "Coronavirus?" What do you think when you're reading the morning paper and see the name "COVID - 19?" What do those words feel like?

I find myself also reminded of the age-old question, if a tree falls in the woods and no one is around to hear it, did it really make a sound? I can't help but wonder, if no one ever knew the name "Coronavirus," would the virus still spread? Would there be such fear? I can't help but wonder, and maybe there's no definitive answer. What I do know without question and beyond the shadow of a doubt, though, is that belief manifests. What you think will always be brought into the natural, physical world, if you focus upon it and place upon it your extended focus. Right now, as of the time of this writing, I look to the once busy streets below - the streets that only days ago were filled with people having their morning coffee while they took their dogs for walks. Now those streets aren't as busy. But the sun is still shining. It's so beautiful out. I've never seen the sky so blue and so beautiful.

My friend and fellow seeker, hear me when I say you have a choice on what you focus on. You have a choice where your thoughts are concerned. You can choose where to place your attention. And, above all, you can choose to fear or you can choose to live in peace - not only in times of global pandemic but in all the days of your life. Right now, in this moment of time, the Holy Spirit is attempting to remind us all of the power of our thoughts. Right now, though the virus is real, we can still choose the thoughts we think. Yes; there's power in a name.

The word "name," in Hebrew, literally can be translated as "nature." When a "name" was given, a "nature" was being established and defined as certain meanings were set and as definition was given. Suffice it to say that names bring with them definition, according to our thoughts and beliefs. When Abram's name was changed to Abraham, he became the father of many nations. Jacob, the "deceiver" lived up to his name on multiple occasions. Names brought definition, and, to some degree, it seems the ancients believed this even more than most seem to believe it today. The ancients regarded the power of the spoken word because they realized the power of thoughts and belief.

And so what does this have to do with the heavenly laws? You, my friend and fellow seeker, have been given the power to actually "name" your life and to "name" the world around you. As a result, you've been given the power to create your very own nature. Your beliefs and your thoughts possess power to not only change the course of your life but also possess the creative power of God to change literal atmospheres. Do you desire to better understand the prophetic power residing within your thoughts? Do you truly want to know how to define the Law of Attraction where the Kingdom of God is concerned? If so, begin by recognizing that you're always constantly naming your life according to your thoughts.

We use terms like "good" and "bad." We use terms such as "good" and "evil." Think of it for a moment. When was the last time you heard someone say when something seemed to be so negative and so adverse, "That's an attack of the devil?" The way you choose to define your life will always direct the outcome of your life. I pray that you could receive that revelation into your spirit and into your thoughts. When you realize that you've been given the power to name the things, the events, the situations in your life, you'll realize how important it is to change your beliefs.

Even in the very beginning of it all, names mattered, and names brought definition. Picture this. Envision it. Long before the Creator spoke into existence the worlds and all that would come to be, an image - an inner picture existed within the Divine Mind. There was a blueprint - an inner model. The Creator didn't create haphazardly, and He most certainly didn't create on a whim, out of boredom. It was planned. There was thought. There as intent.

Suffice it to say that Creation was intentional. And it still is. After the Creator spoke, the resulting manifestation that emerged was so precise and so in alignment with the inner vision He held that He exclaimed how very "good" it all was. In this very instant of Creation, we see the crux of the heavenly Law of Attraction at work within the cosmos. Attraction is the principle through which Creation was manifested, as the Creator, through His very own, willful intent, envisioned the world and all that would be within it. Yes, in the very beginning of it all, God spoke; however, long, long before God spoke, He first thought. Everything that you see in existence even now exists solely because the Creator thought.

Being that man was created in the very image and in the very likeness of God, man, too, possessed this same creative power. As man became a living, breathing soul, man took on the very essence of the Creator, becoming infused with the same creative power and the same ability to think, to reason, to envision, and to dream. The dominion given to man within the Garden Paradise wasn't some mystical force suddenly imparted unto him from on high. No; it was merely an extension of man's very own identity - that of Creator. Today, the very same principle applies and it always will. Just as the Creator spoke, He's still speaking. And just as the Creator thought, He's still thinking. And you, with every passing thought, are but an emanation of that same Divine Mind.

The Divine Mind of God is the Divine Mind of man, and such a claim isn't shocking - at least, it should not be. Such a claim is not blasphemous. It isn't heresy to say that man possesses the same attributes as the Creator Himself. After all, as the scriptures make perfect clear, even as He is, so are we in this present world. As He is, so are we.

And as man was placed into the newly formed realm of physicality, he was given also a tremendous responsibility. He was entrusted with the task of actually "naming" the newly formed Creation. The names given by Adam were the names that would define the very natures of the animals and of all the existence of the surrounding, natural world within the physical realm of earth. I share this to say, my friend and fellow seeker, you've always been "naming" all aspects of your very own life, all along, even when you may not have been aware of it consciously. You've always possessed the power to declare and to define - to bring definition into your very own life.

And so what of the life that doesn't seem to be so "good?" That life is just as you've claimed it to be. That which you call "good" is good. And that which you call "bad" is just as you've claimed it to be. And so, knowing this, how much more vitally important is it to fully understand the realm of your own thoughts? How much more crucial is it that you begin to become more aware of how truly defining your thoughts are? A God-life is a life that is "good." *"Do not err, my beloved brethren.*

Every good gift and every perfect gift is from above, and cometh down from the

Father of lights, with whom is no variableness, neither shadow of turning.

Of his own will begat he us with the word of truth, that we should be a kind of firstfruits of his creatures.

Wherefore, my beloved brethren, let every man be swift to hear, slow to speak, slow to wrath:

For the wrath of man worketh not the righteousness of God.

Wherefore lay apart all filthiness and superfluity of naughtiness, and receive with meekness the engrafted word, which is able to save your souls.

But be ye doers of the word, and not hearers only, deceiving your own selves.

For if any be a hearer of the word, and not a doer, he is like unto a man beholding his natural face in a glass:

For he beholdeth himself, and goeth his way, and straightway forgetteth what manner of man he was.

But whoso looketh into the perfect law of liberty, and continueth therein, he being not a forgetful hearer, but a doer of the work, this man shall be blessed in his deed.

If any man among you seem to be religious, and bridleth not his tongue, but deceiveth his own heart, this man's religion is vain.

Pure religion and undefiled before God and the Father is this, To visit the fatherless and widows in their affliction, and to keep himself unspotted from the world." (James 1:16-27 KJV)

As the writer of the Book of James illustrates, everything that is "good" has come from above from God. How interesting is it to note, though, that within the same context of defining "good," the writer of the Book of James also speaks of the importance of faith? The writer, in defining the "good," speaks also of the power of belief and of thought, noting that faith without works is dead. Faith devoid of action is not true faith at all. To put it more plainly, if one claims to have faith and belief without assuming personal responsibility, the faith is not true faith at all and the self-professed believer is hypocritical.

Belief isn't enough. Awareness of your belief is key.

It isn't enough for you to simply believe, contrary to the teachings of organized religion. In fact, it's never been enough. Believe what? Beliefs, as you well know are as diverse and as varied as ever. It's not enough to simply believe; you must know exactly what you believe and, even more importantly, why you believe what you claim to believe. And if you aren't willing to become aware of your belief then your belief, by definition, isn't true belief at all - and it isn't genuine faith.

Now, as you become more aware of what can only be described as true Kingdom authority the heavenly Law of Attraction - the time has come to stop making excuses. Your life is the result of not only your thoughts but also the result of the many labels, the definitions, and the many programmed filters you've chosen to place upon it. If it doesn't feel "good," then something is out of alignment, and I assure you it isn't the Creator. The element of misalignment lies within your very own thoughts and beliefs. You can have a good life. You can have a God life. You can have the life of God being enacted throughout the realm of physicality. In fact, you already do and always have; you simply haven't believed it.

CHAPTER SIX
THE VISIBLE AND INVISIBLE

There have always been unseen forces at work all around you; however, none of these forces have ever truly been apart from you and they most certainly haven't been beyond your control. In order to better understand the truth regarding the heavenly power you've been given as both an attractor and creator, it's essential that you recognize the source of these unseen forces. There is truly a realm beyond that which we see with our natural eyes and, surprisingly, science continues to confirm this truth all the more each and every day. If you truly desire to better understand the role you've been given to play within Creation, it's time to begin to develop a better, more heightened sense of discernment and sensitivity to the invisible realms. There is an invisible realm, and it is the realm of thought forms.

When I began to become more aware of my own prophetic gifting all those years ago, I quickly began to realize that to better understand the prophetic I needed a better understanding of the Divine Mind - the mind of the Creator within humanity. In fact the Divine

Mind of God and the mind of man are so divinely and and so intricately interconnected that it's impossible to separate the two. Remember, as He is, so are you. Knowing this, it becomes even more crucial that you become aware of the far-reaching, progressive, ever-expanding realm of your thoughts. Like the ripples of the stone cast into the pond, so, too, are the effects of your thoughts. Not only is your day created by the thoughts you think, the truth of the matter is that today you are experiencing also the ripples effects of the thoughts of yesterday. The thoughts of yesterday still remain, and it's time you fully realized it. Allow me to explain.

Just as Creation is progressive in nature and continues to evolve and expand, so, too, do the thoughts we think. No one suddenly wakes up one day and decides, "I hate my life." It doesn't work that way. Dissatisfaction and discontentment doesn't suddenly, miraculously just begin in a single instance of time. No; it all started somewhere in the past - in past thoughts - more slowly and in a much more subtle way. Maybe it started when you felt pressured to take the job you never really wanted to take. Maybe it began, slowly, when you decided to stay in the relationship that you weren't truly satisfied in. Maybe it began when you were told by your church that you shouldn't ask all of those questions you kept asking - when you were told, "Just have faith." You see, somewhere along the way, in subtle ways, you began to give up control of your own life and, seemingly, removed yourself from the role of active participant to become a spectator. However, even then, in all those moments of time, you were creating something with your thoughts, your beliefs, and even with those feelings and emotions.

To better understand the heavenly Law of Attraction, it's important to begin to become more aware of the very real invisible realm which is constantly fueling every waking moment of your life. These powerful, unseen, invisible forces of thought have always been working for you, even when it may have seemed that they were working against you. These forces of powerful, creative intent have been working for you by giving you exactly what you think. As I shared within my book *Creating with Your Thoughts*, where the mind goes, energy will always flow. This has always been the case.

The Universe is at Your Command, you see, isn't just a catchy title to my bestselling book; it's a very real statement of truth. Heaven and the realm of earth have always, always worked in tandem, together, to bring to you your every desire according to your thoughts and beliefs. For most, though, where the feeling of "bad" comes into play is that they've never truly recognized that they were always in control the entire time. Hence, personal responsibility. When awakening comes and when the natural, religious mind becomes renewed to the Divine Mind, suddenly we become more able to see the role we've been given to play within all of Creation. We become more aware of the unseen forces emanating from our thoughts.

There is a realm unseen - a realm quite literally beyond the natural, physicality that we call life upon Planet Earth. This energetic force - this field of creative power - is so intrinsically linked to the thoughts we think that it's impossible to separate ourselves from its force field.

All throughout the day and even into the night, you and I are creating according to our thoughts, and in so doing are also emanating a very real field of force around us - a powerful force that's creative and sovereign. Some call it "vibes."

Some consider it nothing ore than just a "hunch." It can always be felt and experienced, though. When was the last time you actually came in contact with a stranger on the street and suddenly felt those "vibes?" Well, whatever you choose to call it you were feeling the force of creative power at work. Others can feel you as well.

It's not "New Age" or heresy to speak of the force of Creation in this way. In fact, if we were to be totally honest with the ourselves regarding the history of the faith and the true theology that existed within the early church within Christendom, the early disciples and apostles believed in this force more than most would dare to admit. In fact, to the religious minds of the modern religious system in this more modern age, the faith of the apostles would probably seem pretty "New Age" to most. It isn't "New Age," though; its simply the principle of the Kingdom at work - the principle of Creation. As a man thinketh, so is he.

Consider for a moment just how often the New Testament writers regarded the power of thought and belief. So much was shared regarding the power of inner transformation that literally every epistle to the early church detailed in some way the importance of it. "Be transformed by the renewing of your mind." "Let this mind be in you which was also in Christ

Jesus". "Think on heavenly things." Nowhere is it any more obvious though than in the Pauline epistle in which he speaks of the need to have the eyes of understanding enlightened. The message of the early church which began in Jerusalem at Pentecost wasn't simply "Jesus saves," as we're led to believe. The Gospel was and is a message of conscious awakening - a realization that belief brings about manifestation.

Today, just as the early church warned, there is another gospel and another Jesus being preached by a false religion disguising itself as the Church of Jesus Christ. This false gospel would love nothing more than to have you believe that you're powerless and that you have no true say in the matters of your life. This, my friend, is the spirit of Anti-Christ. It is the religious spirit which says, "Simply believe," all while encouraging you to sit on the sidelines of life in hopes that your abundant life will come one day. The Gospel has always been a message of power and of authority - a message of prosperity in all areas of life.

The body, the soul, and the spirit are unfolding and evolving just as the rest of Creation, and day by day you are being born again and being made aware of the power you truly possess. This is why the scriptures say that all Creation groans in anticipation of the manifesting of the sons of God. All of Creation is waiting for you to wake up and remember who you truly are! You are the Creator within Creation! You are Heaven on Earth! You are the righteousness of God in Christ Jesus!

Contrary to the teachings of religion, the Kingdom of Heaven has always been a realm within, and, as a result, has always been much, much more metaphysical than physical. Your issue isn't your coworker. It isn't your bank account. It isn't your marriage. It isn't your dissatisfaction in life at all, in fact. The issue has always been your thought forms.

All that you see within the physical, natural world is a manifestation of thought and belief, and the life you experience each day is truly nothing more than just the outward projection of your own inner Kingdom. Think of that for a moment. Ponder that. Because the realm of Heaven is within you, it is constantly being projected outwardly. However, Heaven within is bringing to you exactly what you desire, because you are the Creator within this realm of earth and, just as Jesus said, you are being given exactly what you believe. Your issue has always been your belief and your thought life.

Surprisingly, you don't have to be an expert in the prophetic field to actually read someone's mind and to know exactly what someone is thinking; all you have to do it look at the life their living. In fact, in every session, I can always tell exactly what someone is thinking, and it truly doesn't even require activation of the prophetic gift; I simply look at their life. Your life is the result of your thoughts. And if your life is filled with chaos, disarray, and misalignment, it's a reflection of your very own thoughts. As the writer of the Book of James states, faith is shown by works which means, simply, belief is manifested outwardly.

Metaphysics is the branch of philosophy that deals with the first order of things - the realm beyond what is seen with the natural eyes. But what lies beyond the natural? Is it merely a realm of angels and demons, as some have taught throughout the years? Is it, as some have taught, simply a realm that we should daily war against? Or is it something much, much more powerful than even that? Heaven has always been within you, and, as a result, has always been working in tandem with you. The metaphysical realm - the invisible realm - has always been a realm of thought and intention, created solely by the thoughts we think. Choose this day whom you will serve.

"Paul, a servant of Jesus Christ, called to be an apostle, separated unto the gospel of God,

(Which he had promised afore by his prophets in the holy scriptures,)

Concerning his Son Jesus Christ our Lord, which was made of the seed of David according to the flesh;

And declared to be the Son of God with power, according to the spirit of holiness, by the resurrection from the dead:

By whom we have received grace and apostleship, for obedience to the faith among all nations, for his name:

Among whom are ye also the called of Jesus

Christ:

To all that be in Rome, beloved of God, called to be saints: Grace to you and peace from God our Father, and the Lord Jesus Christ.

First, I thank my God through Jesus Christ for you all, that your faith is spoken of throughout the whole world.

For God is my witness, whom I serve with my spirit in the gospel of his Son, that without ceasing I make mention of you always in my

prayers;

Making request, if by any means now at length I might have a prosperous journey by the will of God to come unto you.

For I long to see you, that I may impart unto you some spiritual gift, to the end ye may be

established;

That is, that I may be comforted together with you by the mutual faith both of you and me.

Now I would not have you ignorant, brethren, that oftentimes I purposed to come unto you, (but was let hitherto,) that I might have some fruit among you also, even as among other Gentiles.

I am debtor both to the Greeks, and to the Barbarians; both to the wise, and to the unwise.

So, as much as in me is, I am ready to preach the gospel to you that are at Rome also.

For I am not ashamed of the gospel of Christ: for it is the power of God unto salvation to every one that believeth; to the Jew first, and also to the Greek.

For therein is the righteousness of God revealed from faith to faith: as it is written, The just shall live by faith.

For the wrath of God is revealed from heaven against all ungodliness and unrighteousness of men, who hold the truth in unrighteousness;

Because that which may be known of God is manifest in them; for God hath shewed it unto them.

For the invisible things of him from the creation of the world are clearly seen, being understood by the things that are made, even his eternal power and Godhead; so that they are without excuse:

Because that, when they knew God, they glorified him not as God, neither were thankful; but became vain in their imaginations, and their foolish heart was darkened.

Professing themselves to be wise, they became fools,

And changed the glory of the uncorruptible God into an image made like to corruptible man, and to birds, and fourfooted beasts, and creeping things.

Wherefore God also gave them up to uncleanness through the lusts of their own hearts, to dishonour their own bodies between themselves:

Who changed the truth of God into a lie, and worshipped and served the creature more than the Creator, who is blessed for ever. Amen.

For this cause God gave them up unto vile affections: for even their women did change the natural use into that which is against nature:

And likewise also the men, leaving the natural use of the woman, burned in their lust one toward another; men with men working that which is unseemly, and receiving in themselves that recompence of their error which was meet.

And even as they did not like to retain God in their knowledge, God gave them over to a reprobate mind, to do those things which are not convenient;

Being filled with all unrighteousness, fornication, wickedness, covetousness, maliciousness; full of envy, murder, debate, deceit, malignity; whisperers,

Backbiters, haters of God, despiteful, proud, boasters, inventors of evil things, disobedient to parents,

Without understanding, covenantbreakers, without natural affection, implacable, unmerciful:

Who knowing the judgment of God, that they which commit such things are worthy of death, not only do the same, but have pleasure in them that do them." (Romans 1:1-32 KJV)

Notice that within Paul's epistle to the early church at Rome, he makes mention of the "invisible things" being revealed. Could it be that the early church not only believed in the powerful Kingdom Law of Attraction but also taught it? The answer is a resounding yes! There's a reason, you see, why the early church walked in such power and in such a visible, tangible dispensation of the miraculous. The reason isn't simply that they existed at the right time in history, as some Cessationist theologians assert. No; the reason is that they believed wholeheartedly in the "good news" of the Gospel - that Heaven is within.

The time has come to awaken to to your true power. It's time to reclaim your Kingdom authority! It's time to walk into the abundant life that's always existed for you, simply waiting to be recognized. When awakening comes and when you cast off the filtered lens of religious limitation and come to the maturity of the faith, you will begin to see that you've always been able to have a very real say in all the matters of your daily life. And when awakening comes, the Kingdom begins to emerge all the more.

CHAPTER SEVEN
CONSCIOUS VERSUS UN-CONSCIOUS

In the beginning was the Word. And as the writer of the synoptic Gospel of John states, everything in existence came from that very Word. To put it another way, though, knowing that there can be no Word without intention and without thought, it truly is no injustice to the text to say "In the beginning was the Divine Mind." And all things in existence came from that Divine Mind - even you. This truth is crucial to gaining a better, more comprehensive understanding of the powerful forces of attraction and co-creation at work. Yes, you are a co-creator with God; however, you are also an extension of the Creator Himself, and just as He is, so are you.

As the Holy Spirit began to impress upon me the revelation that would come to serve as the basis of this book, I found myself pondering the many ancient texts within the Christian faith which seem to illustrate a very early belief in the heavenly Law of Attraction. Almost immediately it became quite obvious to me that the early church not only believed in the power of Creation but also seemed to recognize the role belief plays in bringing about the abundant life. Contrary to what modern religion teaches, the early church emphatically did not believe or teach or proclaim that the abundant life just naturally comes on its own. It taught in no uncertain terms that even the abundant life is progressive in nature - that it comes as the soul begins to prosper, as awakening continues. This is why Paul spoke of the importance of having the mind renewed. And yet even that renewal is progressive and ever-evolving.

Awakening is not some singular, one time occurrence. There isn't some point of arrival at which the believer is able to fully say, "I've awakened, so I've arrived." There is always more to be seen, more to be revealed, and even more to be recognized as we continue to grow into the maturity of faith. There is no ending where faith is concerned and where the journey of awakening is. With each new day and, yes, with each passing thought, we're creating and also re-creating life, as His mercies are made new each and every morning. This is why the scriptures make mention of Him who was, who is, and who is to come. This speaks of progression and of forward movement, in that He is constantly coming again and again, allowing us to be born again and again. This is why Paul also made mention of being moved from "glory" to "glory."

You're no longer the person you once were.

You're no longer the person you were yesterday, and, in fact, even the person you were even this morning has passed away, as all things have been made new in this present moment. Tomorrow, though, even the moments of today will be but a memory. You're constantly being given the chance to be born again, all over again. Thankfully, through each rebirth, you're always given a very real say in the matters of your life experience. You've never been separated from the role of Creator in the physical, natural world.

I felt led by the Holy Spirit to include this chapter within the book because there has always been a far greater "glory" - a far greater authority - than you've ever truly recognized.

It's time that you begin to recognize it and begin to hunger after it and passionately pursue it. I'm not satisfied with the lies of religion, and my prayer for you is that you would begin to hunger as never before for the truth of the inner Christ. When you begin to see Him as He is, you will then begin to realize that in the Kingdom, absolutely nothing has ever been beyond your control as a powerful attractor and co-creator with God. But you're going to have to begin to do the hard work, where your thoughts and beliefs are concerned. You're going to have to allow yourself to change.

Change can be difficult, and change, regardless of when it comes, is always more than just a minor inconvenience. It hurts to change, also, because with change comes growth and expansion. It can be painful to say goodbye to the beliefs and to those old mindsets which for so long seemed to be so comforting. I can share even from my own life and in my own, personal journey of faith that when the mind is changed, the change can be shocking at times. I'm not the person I once was, thankfully - and neither are you. Every day you're growing; you're changing. You're being moved forward into greater glories and into new and fresh revelational knowledge. Just as Creation is progressive in nature, so, too, is the spirit, the soul, and even the body.

With greater knowledge, though, comes also a greater sense of awareness - and with that awareness a new, added sense of personal responsibility. As the old saying goes, when you know better, you do better - hopefully. But what does awareness truly mean? When moments of awakening come, what does that awareness look like and what does the added responsibility entail, where thoughts and beliefs are concerned? Is it simply that we should become more aware of our thoughts, or is it something even more than that? As I've said, it's not enough to simply believe what we've been told to believe. We need to believe according to the revelation we know and we need to know exactly why we believe what we believe. This awareness I speak of requires a new sense of introspection.

Given that all thought is infused with creative energy and that the many thoughts you think are powerful even beyond comprehension, you must learn to become much more aware of your own thoughts and motives. All throughout the scriptures, not only is the element of belief spoken of but also the elements of motive and intention. To better understand your intentions requires being more able to see the inner vision you've been given. What do you want your thoughts to accomplish? This question is really paramount when awakening to the power of thought forms.

As I shared in my bestselling book *Creating with Your Thoughts*, you and I, by divine and intelligent design, have actually been given front row seats to the thoughts we think - given opportunities to actually see each and every passing thought. What do those thoughts look like? Thought is so intricately tied to visualization that it's literally impossible to separate thought from those inner, mental pictures that flash upon the screen of the mind's eye all throughout the day. When you think of your relationship, you see those many pictures of your significant other. When you think of work, you imagine your coworkers or see the stack of paperwork sitting on your desk. And when you think of the abundant life that you claim to desire, what is it that you see?

More importantly, where the element of personal responsibility is concerned, the more important question is how are your thoughts truly contributing to the overall end-result you're wanting to accomplish? If you desire a more rich and abundant life, how are those angry moments, those anxious moments, those moments of low-vibration and negativity, actually contributing to the end-result you claim you want to manifest? Yes; even those thoughts have creative power and are quite progressive in nature. Even those thoughts expand. Even the negative and low-vibrational thoughts attract and create.

You are an intentional being, in that thought is infused with intention. When someone says, "That wasn't my intention," though their motives may have very well been sincere, the action was intentional, by definition, because thought itself is intentional. Personal responsibility reminds us that, as painful and as shocking as it may be to admit to ourselves, there truly is no, "It wasn't my fault" in the Kingdom of Heaven - the realm of intentional thought. Part of taking control of your own life and striving toward the mark of the more abundant life is learning to realize that you've always been responsible for every passing thought. Being able to actually see your thoughts helps in this process. What do those thoughts look like? What are the inner, mental pictures associated with those thoughts? Being given a front-row seat to those passing thoughts offers the opportunity to change our minds and to think new thoughts.

As I shared within Creating with Your Thoughts, with each passing thought and with each passing mental picture, all of Heaven and earth are asking, "Do you want to create this image?" The more focus you place into the thought, the more it manifests and expands - ultimately moving from the ream of the invisible to the realm of the physical. And before long, all of those thoughts that you said you just couldn't help but think have become the thoughts that have overtaken your life, ruined your relationship, stifled your finances, and trapped you in negativity. There is no "I couldn't help it" in the Kingdom of Heaven. This is why awareness is crucial and why the Apostle Paul spoke of the need for the "eyes of understanding" to become "enlightened."

"Let us therefore fear, lest, a promise being left us of entering into his rest, any of you should seem to come short of it.

For unto us was the gospel preached, as well as unto them: but the word preached did not profit them, not being mixed with faith in them that heard it.

For we which have believed do enter into rest, as he said, As I have sworn in my wrath, if they shall enter into my rest: although the works were finished from the foundation of the world.

For he spake in a certain place of the seventh day on this wise, And God did rest the seventh day from all his works.

And in this place again, If they shall enter into my rest.

Seeing therefore it remaineth that some must enter therein, and they to whom it was first preached entered not in because of unbelief:

Again, he limiteth a certain day, saying in David, To day, after so long a time; as it is said, To day if ye will hear his voice, harden not your hearts.

For if Jesus had given them rest, then would he not afterward have spoken of another day.

There remaineth therefore a rest to the people of God.

For he that is entered into his rest, he also hath ceased from his own works, as God did from his.

Let us labour therefore to enter into that rest, lest any man fall after the same example of unbelief.

For the word of God is quick, and powerful, and sharper than any twoedged sword, piercing even to the dividing asunder of soul and spirit, and of the joints and marrow, and is a discerner of the thoughts and intents of the heart.

Neither is there any creature that is not manifest in his sight: but all things are naked and opened unto the eyes of him with whom we have to do. Seeing then that we have a great high priest, that is passed into the heavens, Jesus the Son of God, let us hold fast our profession.

For we have not an high priest which cannot be touched with the feeling of our infirmities; but was in all points tempted like as we are, yet without sin.

Let us therefore come boldly unto the throne of grace, that we may obtain mercy, and find grace to help in time of need." (Hebrews 4:1-16 KJV)

Within the passage from Hebrews, the writer makes clear that we're always being searched at all times and that, yes, intention matters. Motive matters. It's not enough to simply know what you believe but it's imperative that you know what you're expecting your beliefs to accomplish. Given the sovereign, unlimited power you possess with your thoughts, it simply cannot be stated enough that your motive matters equally, if not even more than the thoughts do. The writer of Hebrews makes mention of the inner intentions, speaking of a deeper level of discernment. This heavenly discernment goes far beyond the mere discernment heralded within the charismatic movement and is a discernment that's much more personal and much, much more innate. It's a discernment that you and only you are responsible for.

No one else can answer for you the question, "What do I believe?" No one else can provide answers to the question, "What do I want to manifest?" "Only you can answer the question, "What am I attracting into my life?" Knowing this, how much more remarkable is it the words of Jesus himself when he said the

Kingdom is within? That makes it more personal. The Kingdom is within you - personally. The

Kingdom within you doesn't look like the Kingdom within me, and the Kingdom within me doesn't look like the Kingdom within you. Why? Because thoughts and beliefs are unique, personal, and highly individualistic. The Kingdom of Heaven, according to Jesus, is the realm of intention, as the writer of Hebrews reminds us.

In closing, not only is it imperative that you begin to understand your thoughts in much deeper, more introspective ways than ever before, but it's crucial that you become aware of why those thoughts exist in the first place. Dig deeper. Move beyond the shallow, surface-level thoughts of religion, recognizing that you have always been intentional in each and every passing thought. Realize also that it's alright to admit that there were times when your beliefs and thoughts weren't for your highest and greatest good. Admit that even now, chances are there are beliefs and thoughts that aren't truly serving your goals the way you'd like. I assure you the Mind of the Spirit already knows, as your intentions are being searched. Just as you are creating your life and attracting into your life according to your thoughts and beliefs, thankfully, you can always re-create and can begin to attract new and different realities. Change your thoughts, and you will change your life

CHAPTER EIGHT
THE GLORY

The real "secret" is that you've always been much, much more powerful than you've ever realized and far more powerful than you've ever given yourself credit for. The secret is that for far too long you've allowed your truly unlimited nature to be stifled by the limiting, childish beliefs of a more religious, more natural mindset - and as a result, the abundant life has seemed to be far-off. But there's always "more." There has always been the deep and burning desire to accomplish more, to see more, to enjoy new adventures, and to claim even more of the abundant life. As you're being moved from glory to glory, you're always being given the opportunity to realize the power you've been given, more and more. My friend and fellow seeker, there has always existed a better, more excellent way.

As I share this, I find myself reminded of the words of the Apostle John in the Book of revelation. Exiled upon the Isle of Patmos for preaching the Gospel, in the vision, he was told, "Come up higher." Yes; there's always more than meets the eye. The call of the Kingdom has always been a high calling - a call toward the "more" of God. That is where the abundant life is, and that is where you will find satisfaction and contentment. Religion has always had a way of blinding us to the truth of the abundant life. It isn't just going to be imparted to us from above. It isn't going to just mysteriously, miraculously come. It has to be recognized.

Today, as never before, humanity is beginning to awaken at such a rapid rate, beginning to realize that all of those dreams, those desires, and those visions exist for a very real reason. People are beginning to hunger and to thirst for the "more" of God, and knowledge is increasing within the realm of earth, as new insight, new revelations, and new awakenings are continuing to be progressive. In closing, though, I want to offer to you a picture of what awaits for you on the other side of your awakening. What does an awakened life look like? What is the result of a life having been awakened to its authority in the Kingdom of God? In truth, such a life is not only abundant but also unlimited.

Your true nature is that of an unlimited, sovereign attractor and creator, and it's time that you refuse to settle for anything less than what you truly are.

There's never been a single moment when you've truly been separated from God and, as such, you've never truly ever been separated from your own innate power to create and to attract all that you desire. You've only been separated within your mind, where your thoughts and beliefs are concerned. You're not a depraved, fallen sinner, as religions throughout history have claimed. It's never been the case. You've always been a heavenly attractor and creator here within the physical realm of earth. Yes, there were times when you've forgotten it; however, even your forgetfulness has never been capable of altering your true and authentic identity. Your nature has always been and will always be that of the Creator. As He is, so are you.

The Gospel is a message of reconciliation - a message of remembrance. When someone asks you how the Law of Attraction and the Law of Creation apply to the Gospel, you need only to remind them of the writings of the Apostle Paul. In his epistles to the early church, he made mention of the ministry of reconciliation, saying that ministry is the ministry we've been called to. But what, exactly are we called to reconcile? What exactly are we called to remind humanity of? That humans are sinners saved by grace? No. It's much more than that. It always has been.

In Paul's epistle he states that all have sinned and fallen short of the glory of God. All have missed the mark. After all, sin, by its very definition means to simply miss the mark. I share that not to in any way make light of the topic of sin but to say, rather, that sin has nothing to do with your true nature and it in no way separates you from God - except within your mind and within your own beliefs and thoughts. The only separation has been within the mind, and separation has always been illusionary.

"Paul, an apostle of Jesus Christ by the will of God, and Timotheus our brother,

To the saints and faithful brethren in Christ which are at Colosse: Grace be unto you, and peace, from God our Father and the Lord Jesus

Christ.

We give thanks to God and the Father of our Lord Jesus Christ, praying always for you,

Since we heard of your faith in Christ Jesus, and of the love which ye have to all the saints,

For the hope which is laid up for you in heaven, whereof ye heard before in the word of the truth of the gospel;

Which is come unto you, as it is in all the world; and bringeth forth fruit, as it doth also in you, since the day ye heard of it, and knew the grace of God in truth:

As ye also learned of Epaphras our dear fellowservant, who is for you a faithful minister of Christ;

Who also declared unto us your love in the Spirit.

For this cause we also, since the day we heard it, do not cease to pray for you, and to desire that ye might be filled with the knowledge of his will in all wisdom and spiritual understanding;

That ye might walk worthy of the Lord unto all pleasing, being fruitful in every good work, and increasing in the knowledge of God;

Strengthened with all might, according to his glorious power, unto all patience and longsuffering with joyfulness;

Giving thanks unto the Father, which hath made us meet to be partakers of the inheritance of the saints in light:

Who hath delivered us from the power of darkness, and hath translated us into the kingdom of his dear Son:

In whom we have redemption through his blood, even the forgiveness of sins:

Who is the image of the invisible God, the firstborn of every creature:

For by him were all things created, that are in heaven, and that are in earth, visible and invisible, whether they be thrones, or dominions, or principalities, or powers: all things were created by him, and for him:

And he is before all things, and by him all things consist.

And he is the head of the body, the church: who is the beginning, the firstborn from the dead; that in all things he might have the preeminence.

For it pleased the Father that in him should all fulness dwell;

And, having made peace through the blood of his cross, by him to reconcile all things unto himself; by him, I say, whether they be things in earth, or things in heaven.

And you, that were sometime alienated and enemies in your mind by wicked works, yet now hath he reconciled

In the body of his flesh through death, to present you holy and unblameable and unreproveable in his sight:

If ye continue in the faith grounded and settled, and be not moved away from the hope of the gospel, which ye have heard, and which was preached to every creature which is under heaven; whereof I Paul am made a minister;

Who now rejoice in my sufferings for you, and fill up that which is behind of the afflictions of Christ in my flesh for his body's sake, which is the church:

Whereof I am made a minister, according to the dispensation of God which is given to me for you, to fulfil the word of God;

Even the mystery which hath been hid from ages and from generations, but now is made manifest to his saints:

To whom God would make known what is the riches of the glory of this mystery among the Gentiles; which is Christ in you, the hope of glory:

Whom we preach, warning every man, and teaching every man in all wisdom; that we may present every man perfect in Christ Jesus:

Whereunto I also labour, striving according to his working, which worketh in me mightily." (Colossians 1:1-29 KJV)

Notice that within Paul's epistle, he makes mention of the separation being within the mind - a separation that has always existed within the mind alone. The separation, though, has been merely an illusion of the fallen state - a ruse of the natural, religious, carnal mind that has yet to be renewed. But when awakening comes, though, and when the ministry of reconciliation is preached, humanity begins to become more aware of its own innate power - a power entrusted by God. Perhaps nowhere within the sacred text of the scriptures do we find this any more detailed than within Paul's second epistle to the church at Corinth in which he states emphatically that we've been reconciled. How important are beliefs and thoughts, where our own identity is concerned? According to Paul, awareness of identity is absolutely crucial.

"For we know that if our earthly house of this tabernacle were dissolved, we have a building of God, an house not made with hands, eternal in the heavens. For in this we groan, earnestly desiring to be clothed upon with our house which is from heaven:

If so be that being clothed we shall not be found naked.

For we that are in this tabernacle do groan, being burdened: not for that we would be unclothed, but clothed upon, that mortality might be swallowed up of life.

Now he that hath wrought us for the selfsame thing is God, who also hath given unto us the earnest of the Spirit.

Therefore we are always confident, knowing that, whilst we are at home in the body, we are absent from the Lord:

(For we walk by faith, not by sight:)

We are confident, I say, and willing rather to be absent from the body, and to be present with the Lord.

Wherefore we labour, that, whether present or absent, we may be accepted of him.

For we must all appear before the judgment seat of Christ; that every one may receive the things done in his body, according to that he hath done, whether it be good or bad.

Knowing therefore the terror of the Lord, we persuade men; but we are made manifest unto God; and I trust also are made manifest in your consciences.

For we commend not ourselves again unto you, but give you occasion to glory on our behalf, that ye may have somewhat to answer them which glory in appearance, and not in heart.

For whether we be beside ourselves, it is to God: or whether we be sober, it is for your cause.

For the love of Christ constraineth us; because we thus judge, that if one died for all, then were all dead:

And that he died for all, that they which live should not henceforth live unto themselves, but unto him which died for them, and rose again.

Wherefore henceforth know we no man after the flesh: yea, though we have known Christ after the flesh, yet now henceforth know we him no more.

Therefore if any man be in Christ, he is a new creature: old things are passed away; behold, all things are become new.

And all things are of God, who hath reconciled us to himself by Jesus Christ, and hath given to us the ministry of reconciliation;

To wit, that God was in Christ, reconciling the world unto himself, not imputing their trespasses unto them; and hath committed unto us the word of reconciliation.

Now then we are ambassadors for Christ, as though God did beseech you by us: we pray you in Christ's stead, be ye reconciled to God.

For he hath made him to be sin for us, who knew no sin; that we might be made the righteousness of God in him." (2 Corinthians 5:1-21 KJV)

Now that you've come to the place of awakening, having been confronted with the truth of the Gospel, you've also been given a very real choice. Will you continue to sleep and to slumber, or will you awake, as the scriptures say, coming to the place where the eyes of your understanding might become enlightened? You're being given a very real, very heavenly choice. You can either continue to live life through the lens of religion, believing that one day the abundant life will be given to you, or you can, in this moment, awaken to the understanding that the abundant life has always been yours to create and that you've always, always possessed within yourself the power of attraction and creation to bring about all that you desire. The choice, though, is completely yours. Choose you this day whom you will serve. As for me, I will serve the LORD.

CLOSING THOUGHTS

Change is never easy. It's painful and quite an inconvenience. Change is necessary though if there is ever to be growth of any kind - any real growth, that is. For far too long the Body of Christ has failed to grow because it has refused to change. I say that not to diminish the great and rich history of the faith in any way but to say, rather, that if the scenery never changes, it isn't a sign of faithfulness; it's a sign that you aren't going anywhere. The Apostle Paul, when speaking of the importance of faith and belief, shared that we are being moved about from "glory" to "glory." The English translation of the text is quite the misnomer, though. In the original language, the writing is actually much more transcendent than even that, stating that we are moved from "greater glories" to even "greater glories," meaning that we aren't going to be given merely more of the same. Growth within the Kingdom of God is always progressive and always expansive.

As we grow and mature and as we evolve in our faith, gaining new and fresh revelation, we're inspired all the more to put away childish things in order to come to the maturity of Christ. Maturity demands change. When I felt the Holy Spirit inspiring me to share what I believe to be a timely message regarding the supernatural power of attraction and co-creation with God, I found myself reminded of the the ancient text of the holy scriptures which remind us that what we think, we ultimately are. As a man thinks, so is he. It's a saying that you're quite familiar with, I'm sure. For centuries many countless messages and teachings have emerged heralding that text; however, for most, the true meaning of the message is often lost in translation. Thoughts really do become things, and when a man changes his thoughts, he truly does change the entire course of his own life. It isn't exaggeration or hyperbole; it's fact. Such a truth, though, goes even beyond what many believe regarding spirituality and is, in fact, a vital element within the Gospel itself.

What you believe has always been the result of the ever-changing, ever-expanding scenery around you. You've always been moving, even when you may not have realized it. In truth, no one is exempt from movement or from change. It's the way of life. All of Creation around you is in a constant state of flux and movement. How you choose to respond to change is entirely your very own choice. As with all things you've been given a very real choice where your own thoughts and beliefs are concerned. But when revelation comes, there arises also a choice as you find yourself at the crossroads of life. Will you continue to hold to the old, with its comfort and with its familiarity? Or will you let go of what you once knew in order to lay claim to the newness and to the "more" of God? For me, speaking only for myself, what I've found within my own life and continue to see proven all the more is that when we allow ourselves to let go of those old, limiting beliefs, we become more able to awaken to the newness of life.

Throughout more than twenty years of ministry, I've found myself asked, time and time again, if a difference exists between attraction and creation. Are the two synonymous, or are the differences real? If differences do exist, what are those differences? When I wrote what would become an international bestseller *The Universe is at Your Command*, I shared from a Biblical perspective what has come to be termed the Law of Attraction. It's a term often discounted by many within religious communities worldwide. There's something about the term "attraction" that seems to make the religious mind so uncomfortable - so offended, even. Does the Bible have truth to reveal regarding the Law of Attraction? Even more so, is the Law of

Attraction truly even a divine law to begin with?

So often I'm asked by fellow believers what the scriptures have to share regarding the Law of Attraction and many times sincere believers have expressed to me, "Jeremy, I believe in the Law of Attraction but never really know how to share the message with my friends and family." Well, that was the inspiration for this book, Supernatural Attraction and Co-Creation. The powerful, heavenly Law of Attraction is just as much a part of existence as the very air we breath and just as much a part of natural, normal, every day life on Planet Earth. There's no escaping it, really. In fact, without it, all that we see would cease to be. Though the Bible doesn't use the term "Law of Attraction," there are innumerable passages within the faith that speak so plainly and so clearly of the power of thoughts - Jesus himself spoke of the power of faith in ways that can only be described as revolutionary. What we now, in this more modern time, term "Law of Attraction," Jesus simply termed "faith."

All throughout his earthly life and ministry, Jesus went about doing good and, according to the scriptures, healing all who were oppressed of the devil because God was with him according to the Book of Acts. As the onlookers continued to see the many, many notable miracles, signs, and wonders, many wondered by what force - by what "authority" he acted. In answering, Jesus spoke continuously, time and time again, of the inner Kingdom, speaking of belief and of the realm within. Religion, throughout the centuries, has always had a way of causing humanity to look outwardly rather than inwardly - contrary to the teachings of Jesus and contrary to the teachings of the early church.

Throughout the years, as I've studied not only the ancient text of the Christian faith and also the writings of the early church fathers but also the various ancient texts of other religions, what I've found is that all throughout history, mankind has longed to better understand the role the mind plays in daily life. Are we simply here to be tossed about upon the waves of chance, having no real say in the matters of life? Or are we, instead, as Jesus said, given exactly what we believe? What I know to be true is that the time has come to put away childish things where the faith is concerned; the time has come to grow into maturity in Christ. With a greater level of maturity, though, comes also a greater sense of personal responsibility. The Gospel the good news of the message of the Kingdom of God - has always been a message of personal responsibility, at its very core. With the message of the Kingdom has always come a very real, very present promise - that of an abundant life. If you're given the results of your beliefs and if every belief manifests within the natural world, isn't it vital that you gain a better understanding of the power of your own beliefs? Moreover, isn't it vital that you know what you believe? As I've said for years, when you change your thoughts you will change your life. Shockingly, though, when you become awakened to the limitless power of the Christ within you, not only can you change your own life but you can, in turn, change the entirety of the world around you. That, my friend, is very, very good news.

You've always been much more powerful than you've ever realized and much, much more powerful than you've ever given yourself credit for. Day by day, little by little, you're realizing all the more just how truly powerful your thoughts are. You're realizing that your thoughts have such an impact on your daily experience. And little by little, day by day, you're beginning to see just how much of a role you've been given to play within your very own life. As awakening comes and as you continue to be born again, all over again each day, you begin to see, even more so, that all of those dreams and desires - all those visions - of yours have never really gone away. In fact, for the most part, they've only gotten stronger. Your dream of a more abundant, more satisfying life continues to haunt you, it seems, and there is no escaping your own desire for "more." This desire is the very nature of God within you. The nature of God is expansiveness, just as the thoughts we think are expansive. Yes; all of Creation is moving and progressing. Even our thoughts grow.

The life that you now experience is the direct result of your thoughts - both present and past thoughts. The life that you now live is the product of every moment, every decision, every action, and every passing instance of time. Behind all of those moments, though, were thoughts and beliefs. Your thoughts mattered not only in that they were very important, but they mattered in that they literally, physically, tangibly manifested. The beliefs and the thoughts that you gave focus to expanded and grew in such a way that they actually materialized. To say that thoughts become things is in no way an exaggeration.

Could it be that even the ancients regarded the heavenly Law of Attraction and the Law of Creation as powerful forces at work within existence, even though they may never have actually used the terms to define these cosmic forces? Could it be that all throughout history, mankind has recognized in some way the power to create, even when man has used different terms? What I've come to realize is the early church not only regarded the Law of Attraction but that the divine law was actually a central theme even in the preaching of the Gospel early on. When Paul spoke of the importance of having the mind renewed, he was speaking of something much greater than just mere positive affirmation. He was speaking, in fact, of divine law. There is a reason, you see, why awakening is so crucial within the Body of Christ. It's because when the mind is renewed, it begins to remember; it begins to access greater truth and greater revelation. It begins to allow for growth and expansion. And the scenery begins to change.

ABOUT THE AUTHOR

Dr. Jeremy Lopez is Founder and President of Identity Network and Now Is Your Moment. Identity Network is one of the world's leading prophetic resource sites, offering books, teachings, and courses to a global audience. For more than thirty years, Dr. Lopez has been considered a pioneering voice within the field of the prophetic arts and his proven strategies for success coaching are now being implemented by various training groups and faith groups throughout the world. Dr. Lopez is the author of more than forty books, including his international bestselling books The Universe is at Your Command and Creating with Your Thoughts. Throughout his career, he has spoken prophetically into the lives of heads of business as well as heads of state. He has ministered to Governor Bob Riley of the State of Alabama, Prime Minister Benjamin Netanyahu, and Shimon Peres. Dr. Lopez continues to be a highly-sought conference teacher and host, speaking on the topics of human potential, spirituality, and self-empowerment.

ADDITIONAL WORKS

Prophetic Transformation

The Universe is at Your Command: Vibrating the Creative Side of God

Creating with Your Thoughts

Creating Your Soul Map: Manifesting the Future You with a Vision Board

Creating Your Soul Map: A Visionary Workbook

Abandoned to Divine Destiny

The Law of Attraction: Universal Power of Spirit

Prayer: Think Without Ceasing

Synchronicities: God's Universal Tools

The New Season is Coming

How Does God Speak?

What Doesn't Kill You Makes You Stronger

Made in the USA
Columbia, SC
26 November 2022